Life Skills and Career Coaching for Teens

by the same author

Life Coaching for Kids
A Practical Manual to Coach Children and Young People
to Success, Well-being and Fulfilment
ISBN 978 1 84905 982 4
eISBN 978 0 85700 884 8

E-Safety for the i-Generation
Combating the Misuse and Abuse of Technology in Schools
ISBN 978 1 84905 944 2
eISBN 978 0 85700 774 2

Surviving Girlhood
Building Positive Relationships, Attitudes and Self-Esteem to
Prevent Teenage Girl Bullying
ISBN 978 1 84905 925 1
eISBN 978 0 85700 704 9

of related interest

Making PSHE Matter
A Practical Guide to Planning and Teaching Creative
PSHE in Primary School
Siân Rowland
ISBN 978 1 78592 286 2
eISBN 978 1 78450 590 5

Building Happiness, Resilience and Motivation in Adolescents
A Positive Psychology Curriculum for Well-Being
Ruth MacConville and Tina Rae
ISBN 978 1 84905 261 0
eISBN 978 0 85700 548 9

Life Skills and Career Coaching for Teens

A Practical Manual for Supporting School Engagement, Aspirations and Success in Young People aged 11–18

Nikki Giant

Jessica Kingsley *Publishers*
London and Philadelphia

First published in 2019
by Jessica Kingsley Publishers
73 Collier Street
London N1 9BE, UK
and
400 Market Street, Suite 400
Philadelphia, PA 19106, USA

www.jkp.com

Copyright © Nikki Giant 2019

Front cover image source: iStockphoto®. The cover image is for illustrative purposes only, and any person featuring is a model.

All rights reserved. No part of this publication may be reproduced in any material form (including photocopying, storing in any medium by electronic means or transmitting) without the written permission of the copyright owner except in accordance with the provisions of the law or under terms of a licence issued in the UK by the Copyright Licensing Agency Ltd. www.cla.co.uk or in overseas territories by the relevant reproduction rights organisation, for details see www.ifrro.org. Applications for the copyright owner's written permission to reproduce any part of this publication should be addressed to the publisher.

All pages marked with ★ may be photocopied and can be downloaded at www.jkp.com/voucher for personal use with this programme, but may not be reproduced for any other purposes without the permission of the publisher.

Warning: The doing of an unauthorised act in relation to a copyright work may result in both a civil claim for damages and criminal prosecution.

Library of Congress Cataloging in Publication Data
Names: Giant, Nikki, 1982- author.
Title: Life skills and career coaching for teens : a practical manual to supporting school engagement, aspirations and success in young people aged 11-18 / Nikki Giant.
Description: London ; Philadelphia : Jessica Kingsley Publishers, 2018. | Includes bibliographical references.
Identifiers: LCCN 2018030531 | ISBN 9781785926105
Subjects: LCSH: Career education. | Life skills--Study and teaching. | School-to-work transition. | Motivation in education. | Teenagers--Counseling of.
Classification: LCC LC1037 .G5 2018 | DDC 370.113--dc23 LC record available at https://lccn.loc.gov/2018030531

British Library Cataloguing in Publication Data
A CIP catalogue record for this book is available from the British Library

ISBN 978 1 78592 610 5
eISBN 978 1 78592 612 9

Printed and bound in Great Britain

All pages marked with a ★ can be photocopied or downloaded from www.jkp.com/voucher using the code ZEYBAKA

Contents

Understanding Youth Engagement and Aspirations

1	Introduction	13
2	Defining Aspirations	17
3	Aspirations and Gender	27
4	Aspirations and Ethnicity	29
5	What Works to Improve Aspirations?	31
6	Motivation	37

The Readiness for Life (RfL) Programme

7	Programme Aims	45
8	The Structure of the RfL Programme	49
9	The Eight RfL Themes	53
10	Creating the Learning Environment	56
11	Delivering the RfL Curriculum	59
12	Monitoring and Evaluation	64

The Readiness for Life (RfL) Curriculum

Theme 1: Believing in Me — 69
Learning objectives — 69
Activities — 69
Activity 1: Recipe for Success — 70
Activity 2: Getting to Know Me — 72
Activity 3: My Life Map — 74
Activity 4: Locus of Control — 76

Activity 5: Needs, Success and Aspirations	78
Activity 6: Core Beliefs	80
Activity 7: Self-Belief	82
Resource 1.1: Outline of a Person	84
Resource 1.2: Ideal Me	85
Resource 1.3: Locus of Control	86
Resource 1.4: Needs Triangle	88
Resource 1.5: Belief Labels	89
Resource 1.6: My Beliefs	93
Resource 1.7: I'm Proud of Me	94
Theme 2: Skills for Life	**95**
Learning objectives	95
Activities	95
Activity 1: Team Building	97
Activity 2: Who's Right for the Job?	99
Activity 3: Who Do You Need on Your Team?	100
Activity 4: Are You a Team Player?	101
Activity 5: Problem Solving	102
Activity 6: Networking	103
Activity 7: Networking Skills	104
Activity 8: Interview Skills	105
Activity 9: Agree or Disagree?	106
Activity 10: Presentation Skills	108
Activity 11: First Impressions	110
Resource 2.1: Potential Employee Case Studies	112
Resource 2.2: I'm the Boss	114
Resource 2.3: Who Do You Need on Your Team?	116
Resource 2.4: Are You a Team Player?	118
Resource 2.5: Problem Solving Case Studies	120
Resource 2.6: Problem Solvers Worksheet	122
Resource 2.7: Networking Worksheet	123
Resource 2.8: Find Someone	124
Resource 2.9: Agree–Disagree Labels	125
Resource 2.10: First Impressions	128

Theme 3: Dream Building	**129**
Learning objectives	129
Activities	129
Activity 1: Vision Boards	130
Activity 2: Visioning the Future	131
Activity 3: Wants versus Needs	133
Activity 4: Creative Visualisation	134
Activity 5: Five Years from Now	136
Activity 6: Dream Inspiration	137
Resource 3.1: List of Values	138
Resource 3.2: Wants versus Needs	139
Resource 3.3: Creative Visualisation Script	140
Resource 3.4: Five Years from Now	142
Theme 4: Money Matters	**144**
Learning objectives	144
Activities	144
Activity 1: Does Money Matter?	145
Activity 2: Money Essentials	147
Activity 3: True or False?	149
Activity 4: Calculating Costs	151
Activity 5: Savvy Savers	153
Activity 6: Money Values	154
Activity 7: The Cost of Living	156
Activity 8: Budgeting Basics	158
Resource 4.1: Money Essentials Labels	159
Resource 4.2: Money Essentials Descriptions	160
Resource 4.3: True or False Labels	164
Resource 4.4: Borrowing and Lending Cheat Sheet	166
Resource 4.5: Calculating Costs Case Studies	168
Resource 4.6: Saving Case Studies	170
Resource 4.7: Job Labels	171
Resource 4.8: Salary Labels	175
Resource 4.9: Job and Salary Answers	179
Resource 4.10: Cost of Living Worksheet	180

Resource 4.11: Budgeting Basics Case Study	182
Resource 4.12: Budget Example	184

Theme 5: Influences — 185

Learning objectives	185
Activities	185
Activity 1: Mixed Messages	186
Activity 2: The Influence of the Media	188
Activity 3: Stereotypes and Labels	190
Activity 4: Positive Role Models	192
Activity 5: Being a Role Model	193
Activity 6: Limiting Beliefs	195
Resource 5.1: Stereotype Descriptions and Labels	197
Resource 5.2: Speech Bubbles	201
Resource 5.3: Success Case Study	202
Resource 5.4: Beliefs About Us	203

Theme 6: Career Curves — 207

Learning objectives	207
Activities	207
Activity 1: The World of Work	208
Activity 2: A Job For Life	210
Activity 3: A Day in the Life Of…	211
Activity 4: Career Stereotypes	213
Activity 5: Gender Stereotypes	215
Activity 6: Types of Work	216
Activity 7: Career Pros and Cons	218
Activity 8: Skills for the Job	220
Activity 9: The Path to Success	222
Resource 6.1: A Job for Life	224
Resource 6.2: Career Stereotypes	225
Resource 6.3: Types of Work Descriptions	232
Resource 6.4: Job Profiles	234
Resource 6.5: Job Role Case Studies	236

Resource 6.6: Workplace Skills Labels	238
Resource 6.7: Job Role Labels	242
Resource 6.8: The Path to Success	248

Theme 7: Business Basics — 249

Learning objectives	249
Activities	249
Activity 1: Who Is an Entrepreneur?	250
Activity 2: Budgets and Profits	252
Activity 3: Big Business	254
Activity 4: SWOT Analysis	255
Activity 5: Profit and Loss	257
Activity 6: The Branding Game	258
Resource 7.1: Entrepreneur Case Study	260
Resource 7.2: Entrepreneur Profile	262
Resource 7.3: Budget Planner	263
Resource 7.4: Business Jargon	264
Resource 7.5: Business Case Study	266
Resource 7.6: Business Budget	267

Theme 8: Ignition — 270

Learning objectives	270
Activities	270
Activity 1: Being a Successful Person	272
Activity 2: Who Is Successful?	274
Activity 3: Universal versus Personal Success	275
Activity 4: The Power Circle	277
Activity 5: Personal Power	279
Activity 6: Self-Talk	280
Activity 7: I Believe In You!	282
Activity 8: Self-Discovery	283
Activity 9: Sell Yourself	284
Activity 10: Personal Mission Statement	286
Resource 8.1: The Successful Man	288

Resource 8.2: The Successful Man Revealed … 289

Resource 8.3: Success Profiles … 290

Resource 8.4: Self-Discovery Worksheet … 291

APPENDIX 1: RFL ASSESSMENT TOOL … 292

APPENDIX 2: CERTIFICATE OF ACHIEVEMENT … 294

REFERENCES … 295

INDEX … 298

Part I
Understanding Youth Engagement and Aspirations

Chapter 1

Introduction

In recent years there has been much talk about the need to raise the aspirations of young people and prevent a so-called 'lost generation' of jobless, underskilled youth from falling into poverty.

It is clear that the world of work has changed dramatically in just a few short decades. The job market of today bears little resemblance to that of our grandparents or even parents, such is the progression of rapid change we are experiencing across the world.

The concept of a job for life is neither realistic nor attractive to young people today, who often seek a more fluid and tangential career path, and the impact of the Internet and new technologies means that many jobs that used to exist are now obsolete anyway. Industries that used to employ almost a whole village or town in some way, such as coal mining or automotive factories, can be wiped out in one closure of a pit or relocation of a company to another continent, where wages are cheaper and legislation less stringent.

As well as changing many industries, technology has created a revolution in the job market. Jobs that didn't exist 10 or 20 years ago are now among some of the most highly paid and sought after, and thanks to the Internet, being at work no longer means sitting at a desk in an office, nor does selling a product mean being face to face with a customer. Similarly, the jobs of tomorrow are likely yet to be revealed.

So how do we prepare young people for careers in industries that are continually changing? How do we provide youth with the skills needed for jobs that don't yet exist? How do we engage children to understand the value of education and self-development and the importance of carving their own career path, when many are being raised in an intergenerational experience of joblessness, reliance on government benefits and poverty?

With over a quarter of a million young people in the UK described as 'NEET' – not in education, employment or training (Powell, 2018) – and nearly 10 per cent of workers aged 16 to 24 in the US unemployed (Bureau of Labor Statistics, 2017), it is clear that something must be done to stem the tide of youth disengagement and unemployment which leads to lifelong deprivation and joblessness.

While there are many efforts on a local, national and international level that seek to engage youth in school and further education, more must be done to inspire young people to find meaningful work and create a passion for lifelong learning, self-development and self-defined success that goes beyond money-making as the primary purpose of work.

Being ready for life

Are young people prepared and ready for the journey of life when they leave school?

The primary function of schooling has been extensively expanded over the past century. Today teachers are often expected not only to impart knowledge on a range of themes and develop the 'three Rs' but also to develop young people's technological skills, provide moral guidance, create opportunities for citizenship and community service, develop young people's creativity and artistic skills, and ensure good health and physical activity. Increasingly, many educators are also taking on the roles of counsellor, behaviour manager and social worker to help students and families in times of crisis and need. Being a teacher has arguably never been more challenging.

As the world shifts and changes, the remit of education and schooling must also. Young people may leave school with a plethora of qualifications and a pathway to university, but may be completely clueless as to how to cook a nutritious meal, pay a bill, interact with a customer, or apply for a job. Some will leave formal education with nothing.

We cannot teach everything, nor should we. Young people have to take steps on their own journey through life to discover, make mistakes, and gain successes by standing on their own two feet. However, to try something new, to use initiative, and to make discoveries requires personal strength, motivation, self-esteem and a range of other soft skills that may simply be lacking in some young people, particularly those who are already vulnerable or face multiple barriers to attainment, good school attendance and positive aspirations.

Readiness for Life (RfL) is a unique, year-long curriculum-based programme designed to prevent young people from disengaging from education and the learning process. The programme seeks to develop understanding and awareness of how to succeed both now and in the future and, crucially, RfL seeks to ignite in young people a passion for success and belief in their potential.

RfL aims to literally ready young people for life. While imparting more knowledge than ever before to young people, our overloaded school curricula don't necessarily prepare young people with the practical skills needed to succeed in life. A common complaint of employers is that young people entering the job market do not have the necessary basic skills and competencies to effectively contribute to the workplace, despite being armed with qualifications and pieces of paper that say they should be well equipped to cope.

Dynamic skills such as critical thinking, initiative, communication and time management are not always given precedence in the rush to ensure young people absorb the facts they need to pass exams. The British Chambers of Commerce stated that many employers had been left 'disheartened and downright frustrated' by poor levels of literacy, numeracy, communication and timekeeping among school leavers and graduates, created by 'exam factory' schools (Paton, 2013).

INTRODUCTION

Twenty-first-century youth undoubtedly need a well-rounded education that seeks to impart knowledge as well as wisdom, and supports the development of children's character and skills. Young people need to be armed with more than qualifications as they face greater challenges to find employment (even with a degree), rising costs of living and more competition in a connected global economy.

Cultural change and skills change

The RfL programme acknowledges the importance of helping young people at risk of disengagement from education, *before* they disengage, by providing the tools and support they need to succeed. This preventative approach is a unique blend of cultural change and skills change, with the understanding that both are needed to generate lasting and effective change.

'Cultural change' here refers to the development of young people's 'cultural capital': their attitudes, values, aspirations and sense of self-efficacy, and exploring the impact of those influences on their actions and behaviours. 'Skills change' refers to the development of young people's practical competencies including their literacy and numeracy skills, presentation and public speaking skills, digital skills, team-working, planning and organisation skills, and so forth.

By focusing on shifting both a person's cultural and skills capital, RfL equips participants with the knowledge, understanding and tools they need to succeed, whether that relates to applying to university, securing a job, opening a bank account, avoiding an unhealthy relationship, starting a business, renting a first home or seeking a reference. These learnt processes will inspire and inform a young person for lifelong success.

The cornerstones of the RfL programme

The RfL programme has been developed to provide a challenging, practical and engaging workshop-based approach to developing school engagement and aspirations in young people aged 11–18.

RfL presents curriculum activities across eight themes, based upon four overarching cornerstones of aspirations development:

- Being Informed
- Being Inspired
- Building Skills
- Believing in Me.

The four cornerstones create a comprehensive approach to building young people's aspirations and school engagement. **Being Informed** ensures young people have the necessary knowledge and understanding about the career, training and education options available to them. **Being Inspired** provides young people with the sparks of passion and excitement about their future, acknowledging the breadth of opportunity awaiting them. **Building Skills** ensures young people have the necessary skills to achieve their goals and create success. Finally, **Believing in Me** provides young people with perhaps the most essential tools of all – the development of confidence, self-esteem, positive beliefs and attitudes that push young people beyond any real or perceived barriers they may face.

The RfL programme is unique in its comprehensive approach. Many other programmes that focus on building youth aspirations emphasise one or two of these elements, such as building young people's practical skills, or providing information, advice and guidance. Without any one element, the approach is at risk of falling flat with a young person already at risk of disengaging and who is likely to need a multi-faceted, layered approach.

Chapter 2

Defining Aspirations

In order to develop policies and practices that seek to improve young people's aspirations, a shared definition must be created to ensure a collective understanding of the term 'aspiration', so that all parties are working to the same conclusion, including parents, teachers and young people themselves. For some, positive aspirations mean striving for academic success. For others, having an aspiration is more specific and goal-oriented.

The Readiness for Life (RfL) programme views aspirations as personal and non-prescriptive. Although school attainment and qualifications undoubtedly help to improve a young person's future chances, there cannot be a 'one size fits all' approach to dreams, ambitions and life goals.

The Oxford Dictionary defines an aspiration as 'a hope or ambition of achieving something' (Oxford Living Dictionaries, 2018). The policy and practice of raising young people's aspirations has become increasingly common in our schools and youth settings, driven by local and national government. Rising statistics of youth absenteeism from school, poor academic attainment, and failure to progress onto further education, training or employment has driven this agenda, coupled with the often media-fuelled public outcry about the lazy, aimless and jobless 'youth of today' which can fuel the fire further. Young people are described as *X Factor* and celebrity wannabes, or government benefit scroungers in the making, dismissing the wider factors at play in this complex problem.

It is my belief that few young people have no aspirations for the future. A 2008 report by the UK's Department for Children, Schools and Families (DCSF; now the Department for Education) found that nearly all of the young people taking part in an aspirations research study wanted to do well in life and had a sense of positive hope about the future, but that these aspirations were not necessarily linked to academic achievement and going to university. It seems that most young people are hopeful for their future, but don't necessarily know how to create a route to self-defined, sustainable success.

This programme recognises aspirations as personal self-defined ambitions, and has been designed on the premise that raising aspirations is not solely about improving academic achievement. Rather, improved attainment is one of many positive outcomes of the aspirations puzzle. This definition of raising aspirations describes a process of supporting youth to define and reach goals, in order to ready young people for life. Through this process, young people are encouraged to set their own measures of success and achievement. They are supported to:

- understand themselves more fully, building self-awareness
- create lifelong passions and develop a sense of purpose in life, over time
- understand that a job or career path can be fulfilling, energising and more than a way to earn an income
- become a productive and contributing member of society
- grow personally and professionally
- develop transferrable life skills
- become ready for life – not just ready for further study or the workplace.

This is also based upon the premise that aspirations will change over time – they are not static, but will shift in what could be deemed 'positive' or 'negative' directions depending upon a number of factors. It is also based on the premise that there are many different (personal) measures of success, including academic, financial, social, professional, emotional, material, etc. Each person's aspirations may be driven by one or a number of measures, which may change over time. For example, a young man starting out on his career path might be driven by his desire to amass enough wealth to buy himself a status symbol of some sort, such as a new car. Over time, the man's drivers might change as he starts a family and wants to develop his career in order to be a better provider for his children.

As caring adults, we want every young person to be successful and happy and to achieve in life, and it is understandable that this often equates to encouraging academic success and supporting youth to gain qualifications. It is undoubtedly true that young people who progress through the education system with a good level of educational attainment will generally earn more and have access to better opportunities than their non-achieving and early disengaged peers. But for some young people, the idea of aspiring to a university degree or a professional, well-paid job is inconceivable. This is simply not within their frame of reference. Many young people follow the life and career choices of those around them, consciously or not. In some cases, their awareness of options can be limited by a lack of diverse role models and a lack of awareness that life can be any different to the perceived norm. Therefore it is important not only that we facilitate young people's awareness and understanding of the options available to them, but that we also seek to shift their beliefs and mindset, giving them the confidence, self-esteem and resilience they need to step into a new paradigm of opportunity. This will create a lifelong path to self-defined success and happiness.

What do we know about aspirations?

Research suggests that the factors affecting young people's aspirations and attainment are variable and complex in nature, with no single factor being prevalent. Gutman and Akerman (2008) state that aspirations are both a predictor and a product of one's abilities, personal attributes, socialisation and experiences, describing the complex interplay of factors that come into play when taking on the task of raising aspirations. The need to take a multi-faceted approach in order to address the diverse factors that might affect the individual child is clear.

The report into aspirations by the Department for Children, Schools and Families (2008) found that 'the strongest factors predicting children's aspirations were: the value they attach to school; their ability, beliefs and prior attainment; the mother's aspirations for their child to go to university; and a family's socio-economic status'.

Overall, aspirations are largely influenced by:

- parents
- friends and peers
- schools
- the media and wider societal influences
- community
- the individual.

In turn, these influences help to create and shape the individual's beliefs, values, perceptions, self-esteem, motivation and skills, which can be the deciding factor as to whether the young person engages in learning and self-development and develops positive aspirations or not.

The role of parents

Children's aspirations are formed at an early age, and develop or diminish over time. The most influential factor in the development of a child's aspirations are the attitudes and circumstances of their parents or caregivers. In turn, parents' attitudes are informed by the society and community in which they live. A report by the UK's Northwest Regional Development Agency (NWDA) states that 'young people's aspirations are being indirectly influenced by their environment from before birth' (2010: 8).

Strand (2007) found that young people (aged 14) whose parents aspired for them to stay in school post-16 achieved Key Stage 3 progression scores on average four points higher than young people whose parents did not have these aspirations. This is equivalent to four additional terms of learning. This expectation alone translates into greater success for young people, but parents and caregivers from lower socio-economic groups are likely to have lower occupational expectations. Forty-eight per cent of parents from high social classes expect their child to work in a professional role compared to only 21 per cent of parents from lower classes (MORI/Sutton Trust, 2006). Engaging parents in the task of raising aspirations is crucial.

Children growing up in families of generational poverty and joblessness, with parents who disengaged early from education or had negative memories or experiences of schooling, will have a higher likelihood of developing negative or low aspirations.

The role of friends and peers

Unsurprisingly, a young person is highly influenced by their peer group, and will likely develop similar aspirations to those of their friends and peers. Youth are highly influenced by their social group, which represents a sense of safety, belonging and inclusion at a period when being socially isolated or different in some way is a risky endeavour and one to be avoided. Being a part of a social group becomes paramount, almost at any cost, and is the main vehicle with which youth develop their sense of identity, mirroring the behaviours and attitudes of their friends, sometimes to the alarm of their parents!

It is understandable that young people will identify with the aspirations, goals and plans of their friends in an effort to fit in and be accepted, whether those aspirations are positive or negative. Two-thirds of 14-year-olds intending to leave school at 16 say their friends intend to do the same (NWDA, 2010).

The role of schools

Schools play a vital role in the development of young people's aspirations. Teachers' expectations are known to be a key determinant of school effectiveness and pupil progress (Feinstein, Duckworth and Sabates, 2004), and schools have been shown to account for between 8 and 15 per cent of differences in attainment (Lupton, 2006).

Schools will largely be the main provider of the knowledge and skills young people will need to progress on to further education or employment and will typically be the starting point for young people to explore the options available to them post-16 or post-18, through careers lessons, work experience, class discussions and so forth.

On a more personal level, research has shown that both teachers' general expectations for their students' performance and teachers' confidence in their own teaching efficacy predict students' school achievement (Eccles *et al.*, 1993). Therefore, it is important for teachers and other educators to communicate positive expectations to young people about their ability and potential, in addition to developing their skills and knowledge to pass exams.

While schools and teachers play important roles in developing student aspirations, if a young person lacks information as to how to reach their goals they will be left in the same static position. Raphael-Reed, Gates and Last (2007) found that many disadvantaged young people in particular lack understanding about how they would achieve their aims in life. This can leave youth disillusioned and disheartened, which may translate into an attitude of 'Why bother?'

The role of the media and wider societal influences

The media is a ubiquitous part of twenty-first-century life and is arguably one of the biggest influences on our behaviour, attitudes and perceptions. This may be particularly true for the many young people who are avid consumers of all types of media and largely lack the ability to critically discern between accurate and inaccurate information presented to them, or the validity of the ideas presented in mass media.

Many messages contained in the media are so subtle that they are rarely detected, but they help to form our beliefs, perceptions and stereotypes about the world through repeated exposure to the ideas presented in magazines, advertising, TV shows, social media, music videos, websites and more. One such example is the stereotype of youth 'hoodies' and 'chavs' – a media-driven idea that young people from low socio-economic backgrounds are poorly educated, trouble-making louts who will amount to nothing. For a young person being raised in a community of deprivation, those stereotypes can run deep: their drive to achieve and aspire to success can be swiftly reduced as they grow older and begin to understand the labels that exist. Without conscious realisation, a young person can place stock in the idea that 'people from here don't go to university, have a professional job, start a business', and so forth, echoed by their peers and role models who also live up to the stereotype. Rather than a media-created label that can be removed or changed, it becomes a self-fulfilling prophecy that they are unable to avoid.

This is also true of gender and racial stereotypes, for example the idea that women cannot or should not strive for a career in a non-traditional industry, or that ethnicity is a predictor of future success or failure. When these stereotypes appear to be echoed in the community around you, perpetuated by family and peers, and are unchallenged by adults and school, it is almost inevitable that young people will develop limiting attitudes about their opportunities, worth and abilities.

The role of the community

The community in which young people are raised will play a role in the complex web of influences on young people's aspirations and future success. Young people from affluent backgrounds are significantly more likely to be told by their family that they can achieve anything, and are six times as likely to be encouraged by their parents to think about career options when they are growing up, than young people from more deprived backgrounds (Prince's Trust, 2011).

Young people living in communities with high levels of deprivation are less likely to develop aspirations, thanks to the lack of opportunities and resources available, the lower expectations from caregivers, and the lack of positive role models. Research conducted into the aspirations and attainment of 16–19-year-olds found that class is one of the best determinants of a child's performance at school, with working-class children having limited access to resources compared to middle and upper classes (NWDA, 2010).

The Prince's Trust in the UK (2011) found that:

- One in four young people from poor homes (26 per cent) feel that 'people like them don't succeed in life'.

- Twenty-six per cent of young people growing up in poverty believe that 'few' or 'none' of their career goals are achievable, compared to just 7 per cent of those from wealthy families.

- Almost a quarter of young people from deprived homes (24 per cent) believe they'll 'end up on benefits for at least part of their life' and more than one in five feel they'll end up in a 'dead-end job'.

- Around one in six young people from poor homes (16 per cent) say their family and friends have made fun of them when they talk about finding a good job.

Communities that tend to foster negative or low aspirations and fail to encourage good attainment in children and young people tend to share key characteristics, including:

- poor neighbourhood quality
- negative peer culture
- high unemployment
- poor transport links
- low occupational expectations
- history of economic decline
- a sense that things are getting worse
- high levels of deprivation
- homogenous housing stock.

(DCSF, 2008)

Living in a deprived community will have a direct impact on children and young people. For example:

- They will be less likely to develop high educational aspirations.
- Children from more deprived areas tend to have less belief in their own abilities.
- Children from more deprived areas tend to have an external locus of control (DCSF, 2008).
- There will be low levels of bridging social capital, i.e. cross-cutting ties or 'social oil' that helps to create broader and more diverse connections with people which can provide a valuable source of inspiration, information and opportunity (DCSF, 2008).
- Young people in more deprived areas are less likely to say they are going to apply for university (Strand, 2007).

Children from deprived backgrounds face multiple barriers to success and well-being that must be addressed if the cycle of intergenerational poverty is to be broken. Programmes that seek to raise aspirations, such as RfL, must take into account the social and cultural factors at play for each individual young person. RfL explores each young person's community perceptions and beliefs as a part of the programme curriculum, helping to build awareness and understanding about their community stereotypes, and redressing the balance of negative community influence by introducing young people to a range of ideas, role models and new beliefs that create more positive outcomes.

It is worth noting that affluent communities and high community expectation (including parental expectation) can also have a negative impact on some young people, who succumb to the real or perceived pressure to succeed placed upon them and thus disengage completely.

Youth who feel they have to follow the family line into a certain profession, secure a good university degree, or gain a well-paid job early on in life may feel overwhelmed by the pressure to please others and to conform to social and family expectations, resulting in the opposite of the desired effect and ultimately 'flunking' school and dropping out.

The role of the individual

The external influences that shape a young person's aspirations are plentiful and complex and, in turn, create an internal perception that ultimately will be the foundation of a young person's ambitions. Our inner landscape – our thoughts, beliefs, attitudes, vision and goals, values and all the other building blocks to our identity and sense of self – will determine our future path. Moment by moment we are feeding ourselves information and messages that determine the lenses through which we view ourselves, others, and the world around us. In a very simplified sense, these lenses are clear or cloudy, positive or negative. They either create an optimistic outlook or a pessimistic one, although of course there will always be shades of grey and variations in between.

All of our thoughts are products of our interactions with the world and, in turn, our thoughts create our feelings and behaviours. Our thoughts and the way in which we interpret the world around us help to create our self-esteem and are derived from our beliefs and values – what we hold to be true and important to us. A child who has been raised in a loving, stable household with great support and encouragement and many opportunities for success will be far more likely to view their future and the world as positive, optimistic and exciting than the child raised in a chaotic, abusive and unsupportive home, for example. Research confirms that young people's expectations, sense of self-efficacy, self-esteem, confidence and motivation are affected by their circumstances (Lupton and Kintrea, 2011).

Believing in Me

An individual's attitudes and inner resources are perhaps the greatest factor of all in improving aspirations and school engagement, which is why the RfL curriculum starts with the theme 'Believing in Me', to explore and develop each young person's self-belief, confidence, resilience and self-esteem. While a young person's upbringing or circumstances may have negatively impacted upon their self-esteem or self-perception, the situation is reversible. Learned behaviours can be unlearned and replaced with more positive, self-fulfilling attitudes and actions.

The internal barriers young people may face that impact upon aspiration and achievement can include:

- negative self-perception: 'I'm no good at school'
- a sense of fatalism: 'What's the point?'
- a lack of confidence to learn new skills or to try

- fear of failure and shying away from opportunities because of the fear of setting themselves up to fail

- fear of being different or not fitting in with peers

- lack of self-belief: 'I couldn't do that'

- fear of the unknown or something new: 'I don't know what will be expected of me'

- low self-esteem: 'I'm not good enough'

- uncertainty: 'I don't know what to expect; it's out of my comfort zone'.

Thoughts–feelings–behaviours

By beginning an aspirations programme with a focus on the individual child and their inner landscape, a good foundation for success is created. Providing young people with all the skills, knowledge and information in the world will not be enough if, when it comes to taking a leap, a young person's thoughts stop them from taking that step forward. The power of a person's self-esteem, beliefs and perception cannot be underestimated. A negative internal thought pattern that echoes the unhelpful comments of peers or key role models can be playing on a loop in a young person's mind without them even realising it.

Imagine the impact of constantly thinking:

> 'You're not good enough.'
>
> 'You'll never amount to anything.'
>
> 'You're a waste of space.'
>
> 'People from around here don't go to university.'
>
> 'You're too stupid to go to college.'
>
> 'You're a dreamer, you can't achieve that.'
>
> 'You'll never be a [doctor/teacher/entrepreneur, etc.].'

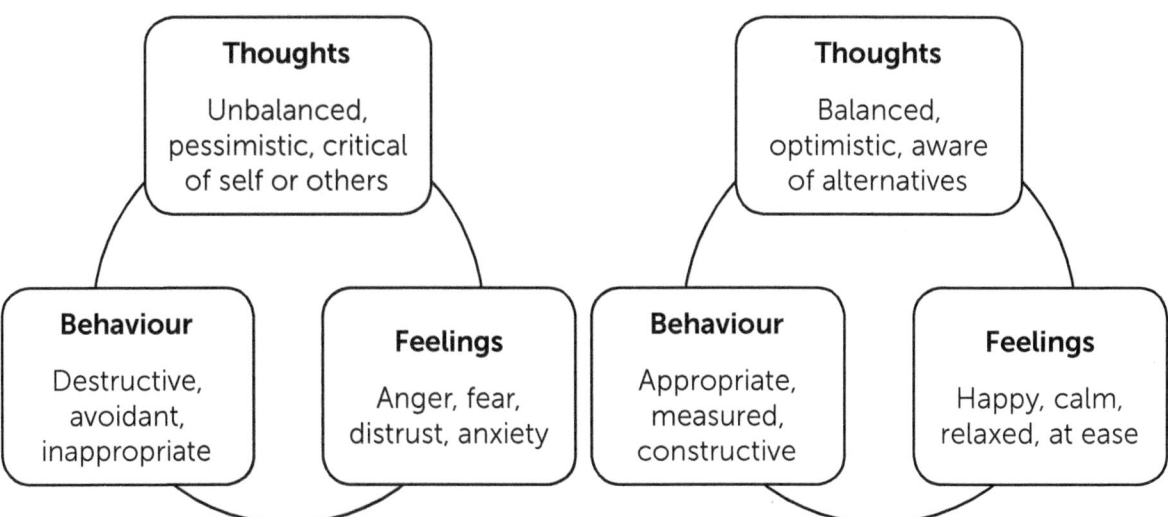

Figure 2.1 Thoughts, Feelings, Behaviour Cycle

As depicted in Figure 2.1, when a person's thoughts are negative, pessimistic and self-critical, they create a negative emotional response that drives a behaviour or action that will likely be self-destructive or avoidant. In the example of a young person with low aspirations, a thought such as 'I'll never amount to anything' can create an angry or depressed emotional response and further thoughts of 'Why try?' or 'What's the point?' The young person responds accordingly by skipping school, not studying for their exams, and so forth. Over time the cumulative effect of such thoughts and behaviour responses can become overwhelming, creating a pattern of thinking and behaving that becomes habit.

Understanding beliefs and values

A young person's persistent habits of thought can quickly become internalised as beliefs. If heard or repeated often enough a thought or thought pattern will become an entrenched belief which in turn shapes the person's perception of themselves and the world. Consider the young person who is often told how capable they are and how successful they can be in life. They create a belief that they are worthy of success and in charge of their future, which leads them to explore career opportunities, start a new training course or apply to be a volunteer to gain work experience. Their efforts to become successful create success, thus creating a self-fulfilling, positive feedback loop which will encourage further effort in the future.

However, some young people are not surrounded by such positive influences, which affects their values, which in turn can negatively affect their goals and aspirations. Values – that which is most important to us – are often created or adopted in early childhood from the messages received from key role models. Parents who value education, learning and hard work will naturally translate those values to their offspring. Other young people need help to distinguish their own values from their parents' or to acknowledge how their behaviours may be in conflict with their values; for example, a young person may value success and yet lets himself be distracted in class and fails to study for exams. Helping young people to identify their values and establish what's important for their own lives can be the first step towards setting and realising goals.

The RfL programme starts with the assumption that every young person is capable of success and happiness, and has the potential to offer something great to the world in their own unique way. By starting with the individual young person, we create a strong platform on which to build the specific skills and tools needed in life. Help to create this platform is the most important gift we can give to youth, as healthy self-esteem and self-perception will last a lifetime.

Chapter 3

Aspirations and Gender

The connection between aspirations and gender is complex. In many senses it appears that girls are much less of a cause for concern than boys. In the UK, white boys from working-class backgrounds have the lowest aspiration and attainment and this is failing to improve at the same rates as other groups (NWDA, 2010). *The Guardian* (2017) reported that in the UK, women are now more likely to attend university than men, at 37 per cent to men's 27 per cent. However, men are more likely to secure graduate-level employment after their degree than women, with the University of Oxford (2015) reporting a 'gender gap' in the jobs male and female university graduates go on to attain within six months of leaving university, with 90 per cent of male leavers securing graduate-level jobs compared with 81 per cent of female leavers.

Ofsted, the school inspection authority in England, found that although girls outperform boys throughout their education, and are more likely to progress to higher education, they do not maintain this advantage when it comes to long-term career status and pay (Ofsted, 2011). The gendered picture of aspirations and attainment is a complicated one.

Women continue to remain under-represented in highly paid careers such as science, technology and engineering and, in spite of various anti-discrimination acts, in the UK women get paid on average 14.1 per cent less than men (Fawcett Society, 2017) and in the US on average women earned 82 per cent of what men earned in 2017 (Pew Research Center, 2018). The gender pay gap (male–female income difference) is in itself a complex problem, with varying factors cited for the divergence in men's and women's income, including the type of job undertaken, the working hours, breaks in employment and so forth. These complex reasons create complex problems: the majority of the lowest-paid workers in the UK are women, with a third (33% or 1.12 million women) having no savings at all, including pensions. This contributes not only to women's poverty but to the poverty of their children (Fawcett Society, 2018).

A 2012 metastudy by the Pew Research Center in the US (Patten and Parker, 2012) found that young women are placing greater importance on a high-paying career than ever before, citing this as 'being one of the most important things' or 'very important' to them, up from 59 per cent in 1997 to 66 per cent in 2010/2011. Compared with young men (58% in

1997 and 59% in 2010/2011) this now suggests that in the US more young women now place importance on a high-paying career than young men.

It is clear that both young women and young men face challenges and barriers to success in a global, competitive economy with fewer opportunities and less job security than their parents. Identifying the gender-specific barriers faced by young women and young men can help to improve the attainment and engagement of both genders and prepare youth for the future. While boys may be at a greater risk of poor attainment and academic achievement at school age, girls are at a greater risk of long-term pay disparity and a lack of career progression in adulthood.

Gender, attainment and aspirations are a significant area of study and could command a whole manual of research in itself. There are many excellent resources exploring how best to engage boys and girls in learning, and improving the aspirations of each gender. Some considerations for schools and youth settings are:

- Take into account the learning styles of boys and girls in the delivery of engagement programmes.

- Introduce a range of role models that can inspire youth to consider non-traditional roles and industries, e.g. introducing young women to female scientists and engineers.

- Teach and model 'soft skills' to boys which girls may already be familiar with.

- Provide opportunities for young women to develop leadership skills and opportunities to share their voices.

- Address specific issues, such as pregnancy, substance abuse, being the primary carer for a family member, bullying, etc., that may affect young people's ability to attend and engage in school, and aspire to and attain goals for the future.

Chapter 4

Aspirations and Ethnicity

The correlation between attainment, aspirations and ethnicity has been widely researched, with many policies and programmes implemented to address the widening achievement gaps between young people from minority ethnic backgrounds.

In the UK, the Department for Education (2017) states that the proportion of pupils from minority ethnic origins has been rising steadily since 2006. In primary schools, 32.1 per cent of pupils of compulsory school age are of minority ethnic origins, with minority ethnic pupils making up 66.3 per cent of the increase in pupil numbers in primary schools between 2016 and 2017. In secondary schools, 29.1 per cent of pupils are of minority ethnic origins, an increase from 27.9 per cent in 2016. Attainment by ethnicity has improved in the UK with achievement gaps between ethnic groups shrinking and even closing in some instances.

Some ethnic groups report significant levels of academic achievement and attainment compared to the national average, such as Chinese students. The success of some Asian groups has been linked to family encouragement and support (Modood *et al.*, 1997; Bradley and Taylor, 2004). However, the attainment of other groups remains significantly below average, including Pakistani, Bangladeshi and Black Caribbean young people. It is difficult to attribute this to any one factor, and rather it may be explained by a number of issues including poverty, social background, and the fact that English is a second language for many.

In the mid-2000s, school attainment was significantly lower among Black ethnic minority groups and those of Pakistani and Bangladeshi origin (Plewis, 2011); today, however, the attainment of UK 15–16-year-olds is higher for most ethnic groups than it is for white teenagers, and a higher percentage of minority ethnic youth go on to participate in higher education than the white majority (Crawford and Greaves, 2015).

When creating a school-wide intervention to improve aspirations, it is important to recognise the social and cultural factors that may impact on young people's attainment and goals for the future. Research conducted for the Equal Opportunities Commission in the UK found that parental aspirations can be markedly different for young people within certain ethnic minorities:

Across all Asian groups, plus Caribbean boys, around half of young people reported their parents wanted them to have a traditional career like a doctor or lawyer, compared to just

10 percent for young white women, 16 percent for young white men and over 20 percent for Caribbean girls. (Bhavnani, 2006: viii)

However, a report for the Department for Education and Skills suggests that aspiration is only one piece of the puzzle, as:

although the participation of students from minority ethnic communities in Higher Education (HE) is higher than for students from white communities, the attainment of those who complete a first degree programme (as measured by class of degree) is markedly lower than that of their white peers. (Broecke and Nicholls, 2006: 3)

It is also important to recognise the impact of teacher perception in the attainment and aspirations of young people, particularly those from ethnic minorities. Asian students, for example, can be regarded by teachers as of 'high ability' whether they are or not, and perceived as 'docile' and 'passive' (Lewis, Gewirtz and Clarke, 2000). Research for the Equal Opportunities Commission states that 'it is hypothesised that these characteristics may particularly apply to "Asian" girls, and stereotypical constructions may assume they are good and well behaved, even if they are not' (Bhavnani, 2006: 46). Conversely, Black Caribbean young people can be perceived as difficult and poorly behaved, and experience negative, dismissive responses from educators, which in turn can impact upon their educational attainment and aspirations (Bhavnani, 2006).

There is no single intervention to help raise the attainment and aspirations of ethnic minority youth and, as the research suggests, simply having aspirations alone is not enough to guarantee future success, employment and good pay. Creating an inclusive school environment, while targeting support to students in need, can help to close the attainment gap, in addition to:

- creating a positive ethos of inclusion and equal opportunities
- promoting high achievement for all
- valuing cultural diversity
- challenging racism
- creating partnerships with parents and the community
- having a clear, school-wide strategy for raising the attainment of pupils from minority ethnic groups
- using attainment data to identify need and target resources
- appropriate allocation of funding and the deployment of staff to meet need.

The Readiness for Life (RfL) programme may be of particular benefit to young people from specific ethnic minority backgrounds who are under-performing and at risk of disengaging. The importance of ensuring integration and inclusion for all students in an RfL group is explored in Part 2.

Chapter 5

What Works to Improve Aspirations?

It is important to recognise that any constructive aspiration declared by a young person is a step in the right direction, however negative, limited or unrealistic it may seem to us. Naturally we see each child's potential for success, happiness and contribution to the world, and it can be incredibly frustrating for a practitioner to be faced with a young person who is capable of so much but has so little self-belief or drive to achieve.

For young people with very negative or limited aspirations, and/or those at risk of early disengagement from education, it is important to adopt a step-by-step, staged approach taking into account the diverse and multiple factors that have contributed to their current mindset and position in life. It is also important to recognise that aspirations are not static, and change is always possible, as evidenced by the many inspirational young people and adults who have turned a corner in their lives, strived for something more, and created success from their disadvantaged upbringing or negative circumstances.

Defining an ambition, no matter how limited it might seem to us, could be a huge leap in the right direction for a young person who has never dared create a goal for the future. It is the first step towards creating bigger dreams, more realistic aspirations or the practical skills needed to create lifelong success, which we can assist young people to do.

When should we start to build aspirations?

Fostering ambition in children should start at a young age, with a repeated and more comprehensive focus as children grow older. Research suggests that 11–14 is a key age range for focusing on aspirations, when young people move from idealistic to more realistic ambitions. Childish dreams give way to more concrete goals, but negative self-perceptions and attitudes can also set in, becoming embedded as core beliefs which are much harder to challenge and overturn.

Research conducted by the Northwest Regional Development Agency (NWDA) in the UK found that 'young people are more likely to achieve positive outcomes when they develop ambitious, achievable aspirations, combined with the self-esteem, self-efficacy, information and inspiration they need to persevere towards their goals' (2010: 7). This suggests the importance of not only broadening the horizons of young people, but helping them to develop a success mindset. The self-esteem, confidence, resilience and self-belief needed to take small or broad steps towards success are fostered across a lifetime, beginning from a young age and continuing into adulthood. There is no key age when building self-esteem should begin; rather, this is an effort that schools, teachers, youth workers and parents should undertake continuously.

Taking a multi-faceted approach

There are many different approaches to raising aspirations and improving youth attainment, including offering financial or material incentives to improve engagement, developing young people's practical skills and abilities, providing information and guidance, or developing a young person's inner resources. There are benefits to each approach, but research suggests that a multi-layered, comprehensive method might be the best approach for supporting youth at risk of disengaging from education.

Positive approaches to aspiration development include:

- exemplifying positive behaviours by introducing young people to diverse and positive role models
- providing trusted and appropriate sources of information and guidance
- creating links between schools and employers
- creating a school-wide culture and ethos of positive aspiration and success
- providing mentoring and individualised support to young people
- exposing young people to new experiences to broaden horizons and build confidence
- involving parents and improving parents' knowledge about the opportunities available to young people
- fostering youth awareness about the opportunities available and supporting youth to be able to access them
- removing the barriers young people face to accessing opportunities and reaching their aspirations, including logistical issues such as transportation.

Cultural change and skills change

The Readiness for Life (RfL) programme adopts a unique blend of a cultural change and skills change approach, aiming to help develop the practical skills and knowledge young people need to positively succeed right now, as well as focusing on the development of their 'cultural capital' to foster lifelong change. Both are needed to enable young people to maintain their positive growth and development in the future.

'Cultural capital' refers to a person's attitudes, values, aspirations and sense of self-efficacy, and exploring the impact of those influences on their actions and behaviours. It is developed by our relationship with our immediate environment and wider society, including our family, friends, community, workplace or school and role models, and the media, government, economy, culture we live in, and so forth.

The term 'cultural capital' was first used by Pierre Bourdieu in the book *Cultural Reproduction and Social Reproduction* (1973). Bourdieu declared that success in the education system is facilitated by the possession of cultural capital and of higher class, and that lower-class pupils do not in general possess these traits, so the failure of the majority of these pupils is inevitable. As researcher Alice Sullivan writes in an article for the *Netherlands Journal of Social Sciences*:

> Bourdieu states that cultural capital consists of familiarity with the dominant culture in a society, and especially the ability to understand and use 'educated' language. The possession of cultural capital varies with social class, yet the education system assumes the possession of cultural capital. This makes it very difficult for lower-class pupils to succeed in the education system. (Sullivan, 2002: 145)

A policy framework for achieving cultural change was produced by the UK Cabinet Office which stated that:

> The extent to which cultural capital affects behaviour depends on two factors. First, the strength of attitudes, values, aspirations and sense of self-efficacy in relation to the particular goal. Second, the influence of other drivers of behaviour: such as incentives, regulation and legislation, as well as the information and awareness we have about different choices or courses of action. (2008: 7)

In the context of youth disengaging from education, the policy framework suggests that:

> the concept of cultural capital emphasises the need to understand the social and cultural determinants of why the individual came to be outside education, employment or training. In this example, the required policy response may include working with the young person to develop stronger attitudes and aspirations toward these choices in addition to more traditional approaches such as using incentives, legislation or regulation. (2008: 8)

Research published in the journal *Sociology* stated that cultural capital is transmitted within the home and does have a significant effect on students' performance in GCSE (General Certificate of Secondary Education) examinations, high school leaving qualifications for young people in the UK (Sullivan, 2001).

Helping young people to build cultural capital, and therefore facilitate culture change, refers to interventions that influence young people's underlying attitudes, values and aspirations and the behaviours and patterns of behaviour consequentially created. The RfL programme helps young people to identify and explore their inner drivers, such as their beliefs and values, and explore the impact on their thoughts, feelings and behaviours, using a cognitive behavioural therapy (CBT) framework. This helps a disadvantaged and potentially disengaged young person to take control of their position in life and create the necessary outlook and mindset to enable them to achieve.

While this is undoubtedly important in helping young people build positive and realistic aspirations for the future, a positive mindset is only one part of the equation. If a young person lacks the practical skills needed to achieve their goals, they will fail in their endeavours and potentially become disillusioned and disengage even further. Despite our overloaded education systems, young people are rarely explicitly taught the skills they will need to be active and employable citizens, such as learning to create a CV, interacting professionally with a manager, or conducting themselves appropriately in an interview.

Although some of these skills are embedded within the curriculum, such as learning to present in front of peers, or learning the IT and literacy skills needed to complete an application form, some young people may fail to note their transferrable skills, or may be put off from trying because of their past experiences, e.g. 'I'm no good at writing so I can't create a résumé.'

The RfL curriculum explores both the life skills and 'ignition skills', such as using initiative, creative thinking, resilience and self-management, to take their ambitions forward, from creating an individual learning plan to setting goals, managing money or searching for a job.

Combining factors, combining approaches

No single factor will create low aspirations and poor educational engagement. Rather, it is a combination of issues which together compound the problem and likelihood of low aspirations. Figure 5.1 suggests a selection of the factors which create low engagement.

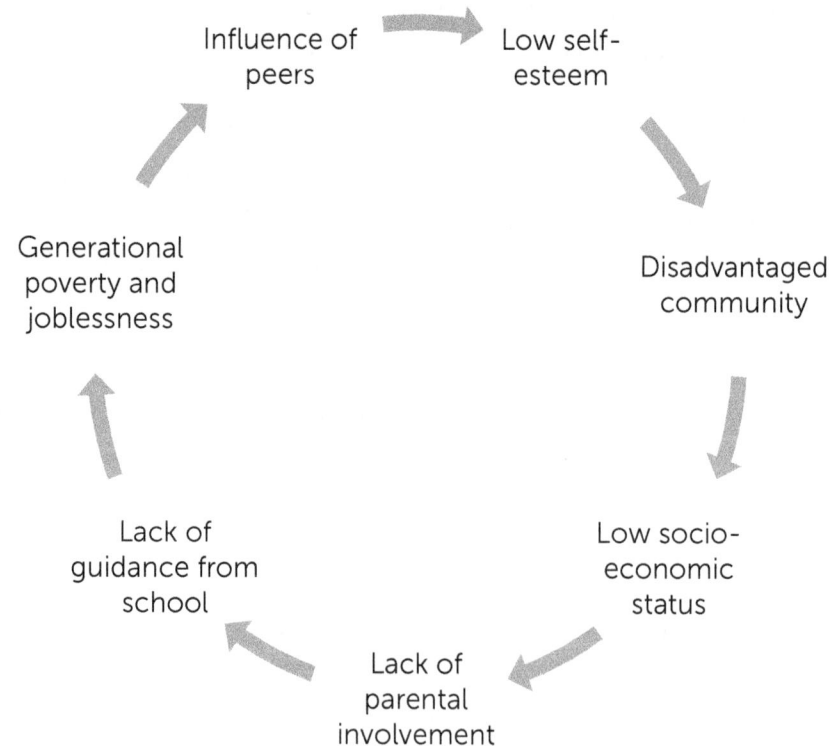

Figure 5.1 The combination of factors creating low aspirations

Figure 5.2 explores the possible impact of those aforementioned factors upon a young person's mindset and perceptions. Although these are generalised suggestions, it is clear that each factor will affect the self-belief, self-esteem and perception of the world, which can in turn affect others. An outlook of hopelessness, a poverty mindset or a perception of a lack of opportunities can quickly become a pervasive attitude as it spreads to a young person's friends, peers or siblings, who adopt a similar attitude. Although there will naturally be exceptions, this kind of trickle-down effect can before long create a school- or community-wide culture of low aspiration and disengagement.

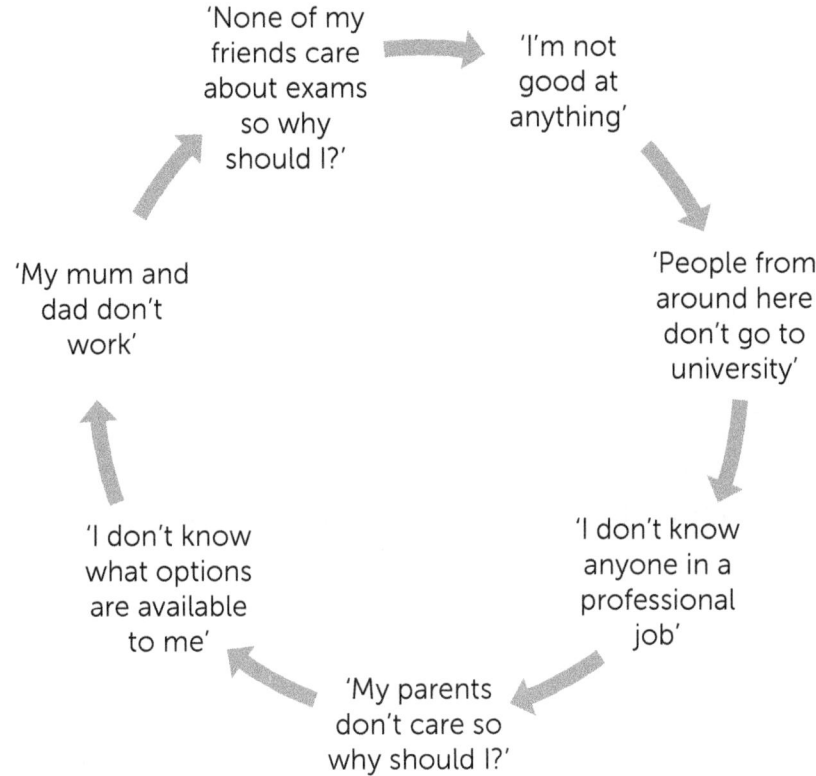

Figure 5.2 A young person's perceptions

Given that there are many factors affecting a young person's aspirations, a singular approach is often too narrow to truly effect change. Just providing information and advice about career opportunities may not aid the young person who is suffering from a crippling lack of self-belief and motivation. Solely exploring soft skills and self-esteem may not help to translate new beliefs into tangible action. Figure 5.3 explores a range of approaches that combine to raise youth aspirations.

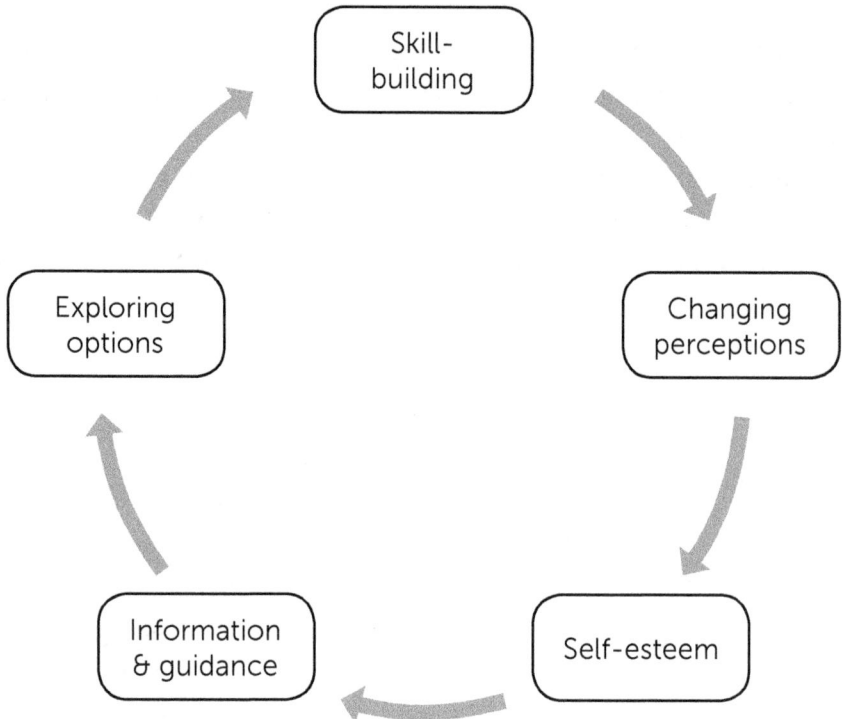

Figure 5.3 Approaches to raising aspirations

The RfL programme incorporates each of these elements within the four pillars and eight curriculum themes which are explored in more detail in Part 2.

Chapter 6
Motivation

The key to success?

Motivation, determination, perseverance. These much-talked-about traits can be described as the keys to positive aspiration and success. Any caring educator hopes their young people will embark upon adulthood with these qualities, to drive forward their success on the path of life. Like any other social or emotional competencies, motivation and determination cannot simply be acquired and learned before moving on to the next skill. Each challenge, each new endeavour, any aspect of life can further motivation towards our goals or cause it to waver and crumble.

However, motivation is not an entity that is either present or absent in our lives. We are always motivated towards something: to get up in the morning; to do well at school or our job; to avoid our problems or seek solace in alcohol or drugs. Motivation is the self-created willingness to do something, dependent upon our needs, beliefs and feelings in the moment. Turning motivation from a negative into a positive force can, however, be tricky.

Every young person has the propensity to be motivated and determined to achieve something positive, a concept that is often ignored. Motivation can feel like the magic, missing ingredient for some young people who are perceived as, and perceive themselves to be, generally 'unmotivated'. Labels such as 'lazy', 'disengaged' and 'disinterested' can quickly become owned and internalised as beliefs by an impressionable young person.

Self-actualisation and motivation

In the context of Readiness for Life (RfL), motivation is concerned with the impetus and drive towards learning, self-development and positive growth, or what ultimately can be defined as 'self-actualisation'. Abraham Maslow, an American psychologist, explored self-actualisation as the pinnacle in the hierarchy of needs (1943). The hierarchy explains the different needs each human being has, on a continuum from the most basic and essential needs for survival of shelter, food, water and so forth, to emotional, psychological and cognitive needs. Maslow attested that a person would be unable to focus on meeting their higher, less tangible needs unless their basic needs were met. Therefore, human needs will only be fulfilled one level at a time.

Figure 6.1 illustrates the hierarchy of needs, with examples of a person's needs at each level. The pinnacle of the hierarchy describes the process of self-actualisation – a person striving to reach their full potential, which creates a state of harmony and overall well-being: physically, emotionally and socially. Our goal for all children and young people is that they ultimately reach this state of being, expressing their creativity, making a difference in the world, continuing their search for knowledge and self-growth, and becoming everything they are capable of becoming.

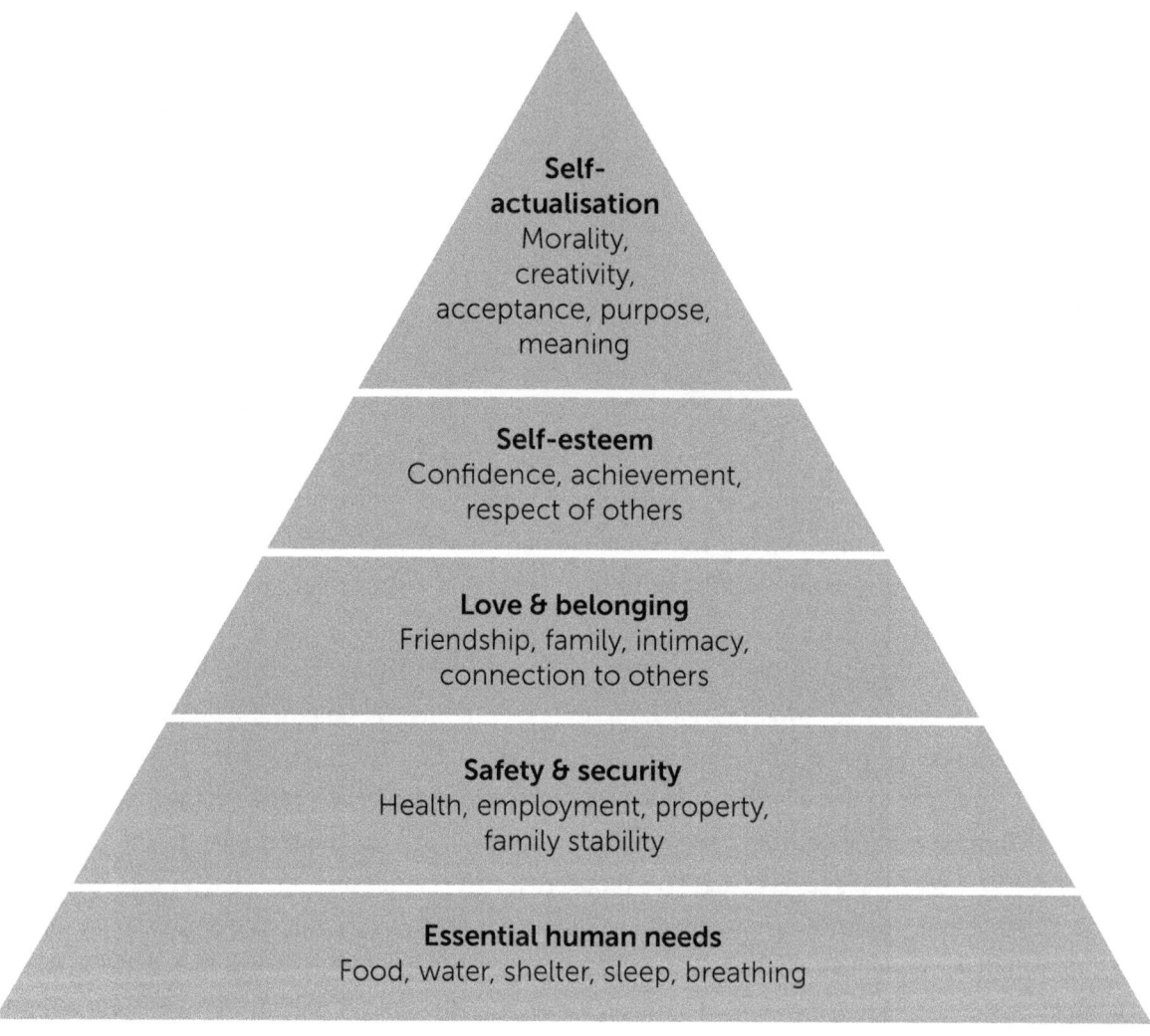

Figure 6.1 Maslow's Hierarchy of Needs

In order to reach the pinnacle of their potential, each young person needs to be supported to meet their essential and other needs. Sadly, many students come to school each day feeling hungry, without adequate sleep, in a state of fear and chaos, or without a safe and consistent place to live. Others lack a sense of connection to their peers and feel isolated and outcast, while some suffer from a debilitating lack of confidence and low self-esteem that makes any goal seem unreachable, any problem insurmountable at times.

To help motivate young people to learn and to stay engaged in their own development – whatever form that may take – we need to ensure they can identify and understand their own needs, and employ strategies to meet those needs as and when they're required. Activities to support this effort are included in the RfL curriculum within *Theme 1: Believing in Me*.

It is also important we give young people a taste of what self-actualisation or feeling connected to their potential feels like. For youth struggling to survive, this can be a completely alien concept. We need to give our young people a taste of the intrinsic rewards and positive emotions that go hand in hand with the self-fulfilling, positive actions of reaching their potential. Small, incremental tastes of the rewards that come with being motivated and reaching their goals create a positive feedback loop and generate further steps forward.

What impacts upon motivation?

A research paper from the UK's Department for Business, Innovation and Skills states that:

> many young people who are not in education, employment or training have had poor previous experiences of education. They will need to be convinced of the relevance and benefit of learning to their lives, if they are to be encouraged to engage in learning in the future. (2013: 9)

There are many reasons why a young person is unmotivated to achieve in school, to find a job or to continue on their educational path. These may be historical, cultural, social or personal reasons, as illustrated by Figure 6.2. For young people who are already disengaged, these challenges can further compound the problem, creating a cycle of negativity and poor choices.

Historical
Family history of joblessness, generational poverty; closure of local job sites; caregivers' negative perception of schools

Cultural
Cultural expectations, e.g. for women to remain in the home, for young people to join the family business, etc.

Social
Negative influence of peers and key role models; lack of social mobility and access to a broader range of social influences

Personal
Low self-esteem; negative self-perception; lack of previous success; negative beliefs

Figure 6.2 The historical, cultural, social and personal reasons affecting youth motivation

Researchers state that there are two types of motivation: intrinsic and extrinsic. Intrinsic motivation is the natural desire to learn and develop that comes from within. It is self-initiated and found when we seek to further ourselves or learn a new skill, or are focused on a goal. Extrinsic motivation is developed by an external reward or to avoid a punishment. When students are extrinsically motivated, they participate because they expect a desirable outcome like a reward or avoidance of punishment.

Extrinsic motivation is still largely used to generate compliance in our businesses and workplaces, schools and homes. Whether it is the reward of a bonus that motivates a worker to put in long hours at the office, or the avoidance of being grounded that makes a child tidy their bedroom, we are all well versed in the concept of the 'carrot and sticks' mentality for making us put in effort. Despite how common this motivation process may be, science tells us that it largely doesn't work. Extrinsic motivation and incentivising people with rewards will only achieve positive outcomes when the problem has a simple set of rules and there is a clear destination or expected outcome. Researchers in the United States found that extrinsic and contingent motivators – the 'if you do this you get that' mentality – may work in some circumstances but for a lot of tasks don't work or will actually do harm (Deci, 1971). Author Daniel Pink states that rewards by their very nature narrow our focus and concentrate the mind, which is helpful in specific circumstances. However, they also dull thinking and block creativity, which is the opposite of what today's workers need to be demonstrating, as more and more jobs call for problem solvers, creative thinkers and initiative (Pink, 2011). In fact, a study commissioned by the Federal Reserve Bank of Boston in the US found that high rewards actually have a detrimental impact upon performance (Ariely *et al.*, 2009).

Pink suggests that the most powerful form of motivation is intrinsic, consisting of:

- autonomy
- mastery
- purpose.

Our schools and education systems rarely promote these ideals of encouraging independence in thought and action, mastery through self- and skill-development, or connecting young people to a bigger sense of purpose in their lives. Sadly, our education systems typically motivate young people by threatening them (with punishments, with fear of negative outcomes) or incentivising studying and achievement, which makes the act of passing an exam or gaining a qualification about the reward gained, rather than the intrinsic benefits earned.

So, how to generate self-sustained motivation in young people?

The secret to engaging young people in their education and encouraging lifelong positive motivation and self-actualisation will not be found in the promise of rewards or the fear of punishments or negative repercussions. Hargreaves and Fullan (2013) state that to create passion and purpose with someone who is reluctant to change, we need to 'push' – assert, pay attention and intervene. We also need to 'pull' – draw people into the excitement, into the vision, into the development.

Although young people need to be aware of the positive and negative outcomes to their actions that are a natural part of life, we also need to develop their autonomy, mastery and sense of purpose to generate the unseen intrinsic drive: the drive to do things for their own sake, because they matter. Activities that people love, that they value, and into which they devote their time and energy, come to be self-defining and are considered a passion (Vallerand *et al.*, 2003). We can achieve this by:

- making young people aware of the positive internal rewards that come with success (such as feelings of pride and accomplishment, achievement and pleasure)

- giving young people control over how they work

- providing young people with a measured, appropriate level of trust to accomplish the tasks they need to

- creating opportunities for mastery and passion in students by appealing to all learning styles, encouraging self-exploration and through extra-curricular programmes

- greater collaboration between staff and schools to enhance the curriculum and learning process

- creating opportunities for success to give young people a memory of accomplishment and a belief in their capability to replicate their success in the future

- introducing young people to positive role models and examples of people following their passions and purpose

- giving young people opportunities to make a positive contribution to others

- helping young people to regularly measure their progress

- creating environments that foster autonomy, mastery and purpose.

We all have the potential to be self-motivated, but only in an environment that nurtures our needs for autonomy, mastery and purpose. Therefore the RfL facilitator will need to strive to create this space for young people to explore, develop and grow their intrinsic motivation; more advice about creating the right environment for RfL sessions can be found in Part 2.

Why care?

For too many young people the future is bleak. Success is a foreign concept, and achievement is for the lucky or smart few, not the educated many. The rapid shifts in the job market and the worldwide economic collapse of 2008 have far-reaching consequences for the youth of today who will be the workers of tomorrow. The outlook appears to hold little hope for a disenchanted generation – jobs are few, even for graduates, and costs of living are rising. School seems to be a pointless endeavour for those who fail to equate curriculum learning with real-life experience.

So what are we to do?

It is our duty as parents, educators, youth workers and caring adults not only to impart knowledge to our young people but to inspire them to connect with the potential that lies within. Having a sense of purpose in life, finding one's passions and interests, and creating work that holds meaning for us provides a sustainable source of self-created pleasure and drive.

There is no single definition of success. It is personal and crafted across a lifetime, and despite what we are often led to believe, success is most rewarding when it is accompanied by a sense of purpose and worth, for our contribution to ourselves and the world. It is the flush of inner excitement and passion inspired by our work and by following our path, rather than solely the material gain or financial wealth that makes success most rewarding.

If we don't help young people to care about their future, if we fail to give young people a practical head start in life, then we are in danger of writing off a generation. We are failing our duty of care.

Let's start a revolution

If we keep doing what we've always done, we will get what we have always gotten. It is time to try something new for and with our young people. RfL is a new take on an old problem. By engaging young people with a dynamic and practical curriculum, adding opportunities to meet real-life role models and visit local universities, building the self-esteem and self-belief of youth, we are creating lifelong habits of thinking and behaviour that not only help young people to create their own career path, but build healthy, responsible, motivated citizens for the future.

Part II
The Readiness for Life (RfL) Programme

Chapter 7

Programme Aims

The Readiness for Life (RfL) programme is unique in its design and delivery. What makes RfL different to other engagement/aspiration programmes?

RfL core features

- RfL is a comprehensive year-long programme, but flexibly designed to be used for shorter periods or within sporadic lessons.

- It is a preventative programme specifically designed for young people who are at risk of disengaging from education.

- It is a unique blend of focusing on a cultural-change approach and a skills-change approach.

- It is a structured programme with progressive themes that build awareness and understanding.

- It is based on the premise that there are many different (personal) measures of success, including academic achievement, status, financial, emotional, material, etc.

- It incorporates practical tools and theory of cognitive behavioural therapy, and coaching.

- It is suitable for external accreditation, should a school or organisation wish to include an added incentive or reward to encourage completion of the programme.

- RfL can be used as a transition programme to support the successful transition of students from Key Stage 2 to Key Stage 3 (UK) or from elementary/middle school to high school (US) by changing the language or facilitation style of delivery to make it age-appropriate. As this programme aims to build a foundation of positive aspiration and future success before young people have begun to form negative mindsets and habits of thought, it can be particularly suited to children aged 9–11.

- Monitoring and evaluation procedures are built into the RfL programme, including pre/post tests for youth, parents and teachers, and guidance for programme coordinators on tracking attendance, attainment, behaviour, truancy and young people's uptake of further education or training post-school to assess the impact of the programme.

The impact of RfL

The RfL programme contributes to the positive development and well-being of the participating young people by:

- improving their self-esteem, confidence, self-belief, resilience and motivation to succeed
- building soft skills and emotional intelligence, including communication skills, conflict resolution and negotiation, personal effectiveness, creative problem solving, strategic thinking and team building
- developing practical skills associated with employability, progression onto further education and training, and entrepreneurship
- improving financial literacy and life skills
- assisting young people to access the information, advice and guidance they need to make informed decisions about their future, and supporting youth to take the necessary steps forward
- inspiring young people to develop wider aspirations and broaden their career horizons
- improving school attendance, attainment and young people's behaviour.

The RfL programme also aims to impact the wider school environment. If implemented as a part of a comprehensive approach to youth engagement, the RfL programme will help to create a positive school ethos of possibility, positive aspirations and success. The RfL programme also aims to address wider social and cultural issues including:

- reducing the impact of poverty and low socio-economic status on young people's attainment, attendance and engagement with school
- improving the attainment and inclusion of ethnic minority youth who may be at a greater risk of poor attainment and engagement
- improving community perceptions and attitudes to education and employment
- addressing local anti-social behaviour and crime, as a result of reducing the levels of disengaged and disenfranchised young people within the community.

Curriculum links

The RfL curriculum links to the national curriculum standards for literacy, numeracy, ICT, citizenship and personal social and health education (PSHE) in England and Wales, and reflects the new standards for schools to promote pupil well-being in Wales, reflected in Estyn's (2018) Common Inspection Framework and the Welsh government's Quality and Effectiveness Framework (2015).

Links to literacy

- Writing comprehensive accounts of various topics, presenting information, processes and ideas clearly and appropriately for the purpose
- Choosing the best ways to present writing using ICT in order to communicate clearly and effectively
- Selecting and organising ideas and information to give a clear and full account of the theme
- Writing with grammatical accuracy
- Writing in a range of forms and styles, adjusting the language to suit purpose and audience, using an appropriate level of formality
- Choosing and using a wide range of vocabulary with increasing precision
- Reading easily, fluently and with good understanding
- Demonstrating competency in speaking and listening, making formal presentations, demonstrating to others and participating in debate.

Links to numeracy

- Demonstrating fluency in the fundamentals of mathematics and applying knowledge to a variety of practical applications
- Solving problems by applying mathematics to a variety of routine and non-routine problems
- Building financial literacy and applying mathematical understanding and skills to personal finance, including the use of numeracy to understand savings and investments, credit and debt, financial planning and risk.

Links to citizenship

- Reflecting the citizenship key processes of critical thinking and enquiry; advocacy and representation; taking informed and responsible action.

Links to personal social education

- Personal well-being: embracing change, feeling positive about who they are and enjoying healthy, safe, responsible and fulfilled lives

- Recognising and managing risk: taking increasing responsibility for themselves, their choices and behaviours, and making constructive choices for the future

- Building knowledge, confidence and self-esteem: recognising their qualities, skills and attitudes, to make the most of their abilities; articulating feelings and thoughts

- Exploring similarities and differences: accommodating diversity and clarifying their own values and attitudes; forming and maintaining effective relationships with others

- Reflecting the PSHE key processes of critical reflection; decision making and managing risk; developing relationships and working with others.

Chapter 8
The Structure of the RfL Programme

The Readiness for Life (RfL) programme consists of eight curriculum themes, underpinned by four pillars – Being Informed; Being Inspired; Believing in Me and Building Skills. Each of the curriculum lessons reflects one or more of the pillars.

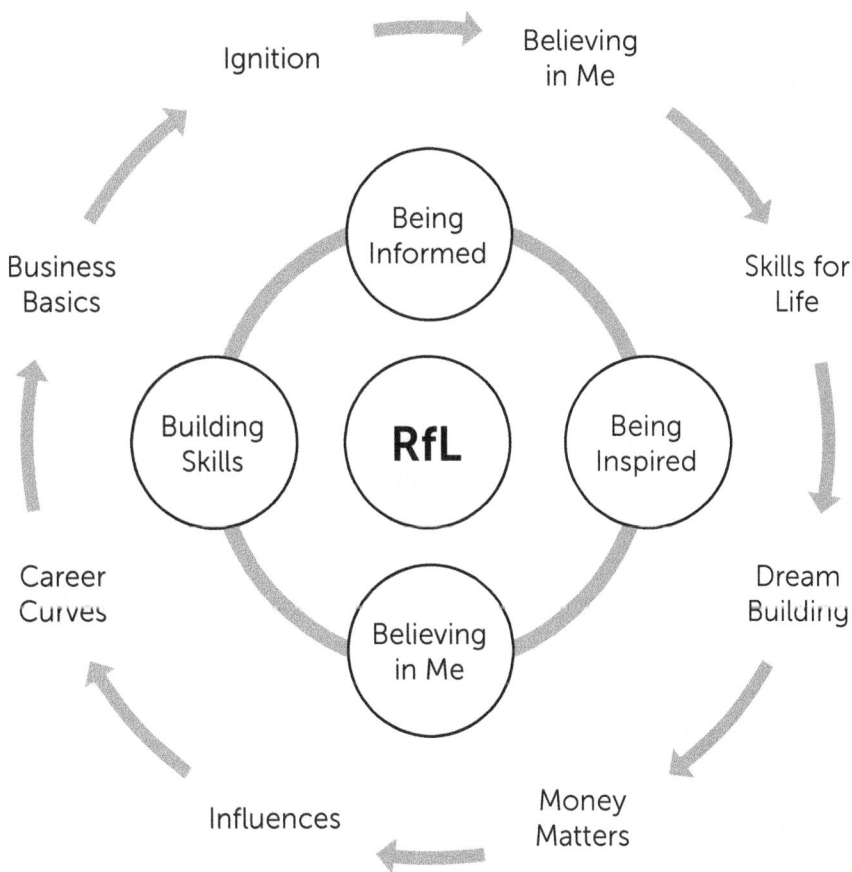

Figure 8.1 Enhancing the RfL programme

If you wish to enhance and develop the RfL programme further outside of the classroom, you may wish to consider organising one or more of the following activities:

- business/university visits
- work experience
- volunteering opportunities
- role model visits
- external accreditation.

The Four Pillars of RfL

The RfL programme is built upon a foundation of four pillars. Each theme and activity within the RfL curriculum is underpinned by one or more of these pillars to ensure a comprehensive and inclusive approach to aspirations. The four pillars recognise the importance of a lateral approach to engagement. When it comes to aspirations, one size (one approach) does not fit all. To build lifelong skills and awareness and a mindset of success, a varied approach is needed, utilising different activities from the four pillars. For example, some young people may need a specific focus on building skills, while another young person may require additional time spent on building self-esteem before they can begin to explore skill development.

Pillar 1: Being Informed

Young people need access to clear, concise and impartial information to make decisions about their future. Unfortunately, careers information can be conflicting, difficult to find, overwhelming or inconsistent. Without a foundation of good advice and support, young people can easily take a wrong path, or fail to make any decision.

Careers advice will differ from school to school and area to area, but within the RfL curriculum there are activities to ensure that young people are introduced to information and possibilities that they may have not considered. This might include:

- understanding the options available post-16/18
- exploring alternative routes to employment, such as apprenticeships
- exploring entrepreneurship
- exploring a range of diverse careers and industries.

Pillar 2: Being Inspired

Without a sense of inspiration and excitement for the future it is difficult to take steps to change our lives. For some young people this is even more crucial, particularly for those who don't have access to supportive individuals who seek to inspire and encourage, or worse, are discouraging and critical.

Pillar 2: Being Inspired aims to encourage young people to find their personal passions, interests and drivers, upon which to develop self-motivation. This will be different for each individual but may include actions such as:

- identifying a range of positive role models
- identifying personal passions and interests
- developing a broader view of the career and training options available.

When a young person feels inspired to forge a new path in life or to try something new, it can be a powerful force for good. The RfL curriculum aims to encourage young people to 'think outside of the box' and look for inspiration in new places, broadening their world view and personal beliefs.

Pillar 3: Believing in Me

Without a strong foundation of positive self-regard, confidence and self-esteem it will prove to be difficult for a young people to take the necessary steps on their life journey towards employment and fulfilment. While confidence is often something that develops with age, some young people will need additional support to overcome internal barriers and external challenges that will affect how they view themselves and the world around them.

The RfL programme includes activities designed to develop young people's self-esteem and self-awareness so they can take action towards their goals and dreams, feeling motivated and determined to achieve. *Pillar 3: Believing in Me* aims to:

- build self-esteem, self-belief and resilience
- enhance motivation and determination to succeed
- address social, emotional and perceived barriers.

Pillar 4: Building Skills

Finally, young people need to develop practical, flexible and transferrable skills that are crucial in the workplace, in further study (such as university), in volunteering positions, and even in personal relationships.

While many young people leave school with a range of qualifications, some will not have learned basic skills that employers are seeking, such as letter writing, communicating with customers, developing presentations or dealing with conflict.

Pillar 4: Building Skills will help young people to gradually develop and practise these skills through a variety of activities focusing on different themes. By the end of the programme, young people should have developed the confidence to put these skills into action.

For example, RfL should help young people to:

- develop 'soft skills', including communication skills, conflict resolution and negotiation, creative problem solving and team building

- develop and use practical competencies, such as presentation skills, interview skills and CV writing.

Chapter 9

The Eight RfL Themes

The Readiness for Life (RfL) programme provides curriculum activities across eight key themes:

1. Believing in Me
2. Skills for Life
3. Dream Building
4. Money Matters
5. Influences
6. Career Curves
7. Business Basics
8. Ignition.

Each theme builds upon the preceding one to create a comprehensive, progressive curriculum starting with the exploration and development of the young person's inner self and ending with the application of their learning to create a practical plan of action for their future success.

The RfL programme has been developed as a year-long intervention to support young people identified to be in need of support. However, the themes and activities are just as applicable to the high-performing student, or can be taken in isolation to form a one-off lesson or workshop. It is at the discretion of the teacher, youth worker or counsellor as to how to flexibly adapt the curriculum to meet the needs of their young people.

Theme 1: Believing in Me

The RfL programme starts with the theme 'Believing in Me', focusing on the individual young person and their inner landscape. By starting with this focus we are acknowledging the importance of healthy self-esteem, positive self-talk and beliefs, and the powerful roles played by motivation, resilience and determination in achieving any feat in life. A good foundation of confidence and self-worth cannot be underestimated: it drives our thoughts, feelings and behaviours, shapes our view of the world, encourages us to undertake challenges and healthy risks, and helps us to build connections with others and believe in our propensity to achieve our dreams and aspirations.

Activities in Theme 1 help participants to understand the link between their thoughts, feelings and behaviours, building self-esteem and exploring their motivation to succeed. By identifying their self-beliefs and beliefs about the world through the activities in Theme 1, young people can explore their locus of control, and identify the triggers to their unwanted behaviours to make positive choices in the future.

Theme 2: Skills for Life

Theme 2 explores the skills young people need to ready them for life. In this programme these skills are focused largely on engagement in education and future employment; however, these are transferrable competencies that are relevant and applicable to a wide range of applications, for the young person to use both now and in the future.

The activities in Theme 2 help young people to build and practise these practical skills in fun and engaging ways, including presentation skills, team-working, critical thinking, using initiative, communication skills, conflict resolution and more. Theme 2 activities help young people to apply these skills specifically to their future workplace, education or training placement.

Theme 3: Dream Building

'Dream Building' introduces the premise that work can be fun, engaging and linked to a person's passions. Young people explore their own passions and purpose in life, creating realistic ambitions for a future career path using visioning exercises and exploring case studies of real people who are excited to go to work each day.

Young people will begin to identify their skills, talents and interests, and explore how their work and talents can intersect. Young people will explore the meaning and value of work, and different measures of success.

Theme 4: Money Matters

Money makes the world go round, and is often the primary driver for young people wanting to obtain their first job and enter the workplace. Theme 4 explores money from a number of perspectives, helping young people to appreciate that financial compensation is only one benefit of hard work and effort gained through education, training and employment.

Theme 4 also includes activities to build students' financial literacy. Despite being one of the most integral parts of life, managing money is rarely explored within the school curriculum, and young people are typically left to navigate a financial path alone. Theme 4 activities will help young people to understand credit and debt, savings, budgeting, spending and earning, by building practical skills to help young people on their journey to healthy financial management.

Theme 5: Influences

Young people's behaviours and attitudes to school, further education/training and work are highly influenced by their parents, peers, teachers, the media and the community in which they live. These plentiful and sometimes conflicting influences can encourage a young person to strive for their potential, or fall at the first hurdle.

Theme 5 activities help young people to identify the influences upon their attitude to work and study, and distinguish between those which are positive and negative. Young people will explore the messages they have received from key examples and influences, and identify a positive role model in their life.

Theme 6: Career Curves

The world of work has changed dramatically over the past 50 years, and will continue to do so. Young people need to be equipped for the curves and turns of a changing economy and job market.

Activities in Theme 6 help young people to realise that there is no one path to success. Concepts such as a 'job for life' are rapidly becoming extinct, and instead youth may need to consider alternative options to gaining employment and carving out a successful career, including self-employment and entrepreneurship, working on a freelance basis, working remotely via the Internet, volunteering, undertaking an internship or having multiple jobs. Young people will also explore career stereotypes, the changing face of women's careers and the non-traditional roles and pathways open to young women.

Theme 7: Business Basics

Entrepreneurship can be an exciting and rewarding career path for those who have the drive and determination to be their own boss. However, the skills associated with entrepreneurship are highly valued in the workplace, too, and are transferrable to a range of applications.

Theme 7 activities help young people to understand more about the skills needed to run a business and the attitudes of successful entrepreneurs.

Theme 8: Ignition

The final RfL theme puts learning into action. Young people will be supported to ignite their learning to make practical steps forward. Young people will explore goal-setting, interview skills and CV writing, as well as creating individual learning and action plans.

Theme 8 activities can be complemented with practical site visits to local businesses, colleges or universities and meetings with a learning mentor or careers advisor to bring their learning to life and hold young people accountable to their goals and plans.

Chapter 10
Creating the Learning Environment

Engaging hard-to-reach youth in a classroom setting can be challenging for even the most seasoned teacher. For at-risk youth, the classroom can become a battleground of wills as teachers fight for students' attention and young people fail to see the relevance and purpose of the curriculum.

Creating an environment conducive to learning is important for all students, all of whom will process and retain information in different ways and need a variety of teaching styles to stay focused. When introducing a new programme and way of working, this is doubly important.

Readiness for Life (RfL) has been designed specifically for youth at risk of disengaging from education, to be delivered in a small-group format on a regular (weekly or once every two weeks) basis. The curriculum themes, session plans and activities have been designed to engage young people and retain their attention. However, delivery is as important as content.

If delivered correctly, RfL won't feel like another classroom lesson. It is hoped that young people will look forward to sessions with anticipation and have a tangible sense of their learning and progress. As the themes and activities are designed to build practical knowledge and awareness, students should be able to reflect upon their development and take charge of their own growth in time.

Setting the scene

The themes and discussion points in the lesson plans may be uncomfortable for some young people and raise issues that might require individual attention. As with any PSHE topic, it is important to approach the activities in a sensitive manner, reminding students of the importance of following class and school rules, and respecting the contributions of others. Students should be reminded not to use the names of other people outside the group in discussions in ways that may cause offence or conflict, and to demonstrate respect in their interactions and explorations of the themes and activities.

As the teacher or facilitator, it is crucial to remain non-judgemental and open to hearing students' ideas, encouraging personal exploration and debate. This will help to foster young people's critical thinking and self-awareness.

Consider creating a more flexible learning environment by changing the classroom layout or holding sessions in a less formal setting. Refreshments can help students to feel as though they are participating in a privileged experience, and improve attention and focus, particularly for students who may not have eaten much throughout the day.

A regular complaint of teenagers is that they fail to see the relevance and purpose of the information they learn. Rote learning to pass exams is commonplace but often fails to engage learners with the material, or to develop an enthusiasm for the subject. The RfL programme is striving to build intrinsic motivation in students by developing their autonomy, mastery and purpose. The development of these strengths lie at the core of RfL. Creating the right environment to allow autonomy, mastery and purpose to flourish is key.

Avoid:

- belittling students, using sarcasm or focusing on negative behaviours and outcomes
- inconsistencies, such as changing the meeting room or the configuration of the space, introducing new students, changing the facilitator, etc.
- micro-managing students or the RfL process.

Try:

- making suggestions rather than offering facts: 'I wonder if…'
- focusing on feelings: 'How would it feel to be successful at that?'
- encouraging discussion and debate: 'What do you think?'
- creating opportunities for student-initiated research and learning: 'What information can you find to support that idea?'
- encouraging young people to identify their passions and interests and create opportunities for youth to become proficient in these
- encouraging youth to track their progress and reflect upon their successes
- creating an equal environment where everyone is valued and accepted
- having ground rules in place that everyone has agreed to.

Identifying participants for RfL

The RfL programme is suitable for any young person aged 11 and over, and can be adapted for younger students. Some students may require assistance with the language or ideas presented in the curriculum, and you may wish to adapt some activities to suit the ability and comprehension levels of your students.

The RfL programme is particularly suited to young people at risk of disengaging from education. These young people will particularly benefit from the full RfL programme of weekly sessions for a full academic year. The programme contains over 60 activities, which could allow for continuation of RfL across two academic years. As the activities will vary in duration depending on the needs of the students, some facilitators may wish to use two or three activities during one session, or spend a longer time on discussion and focus on one activity per week.

It is suggested that practitioners work with at-risk youth in a small-group format of no more than ten students per group. This will allow participants to discuss and explore the themes presented in a safe space, develop relationships between participants and with the facilitator, and create a space for achievement and success.

Ideally, young people should participate in an RfL programme willingly – being forced to attend may prompt poor behaviour, an unwillingness to participate in activities or a resistance to explore thoughts and feelings, which will affect the wider group.

Using the RfL questionnaire (found in Appendix 1) can help to identify young people who are particularly in need of participating in a small-group RfL programme. The questionnaire will reveal young people with low aspirations, a lack of role models, and a poor perception of their abilities and potential, who would benefit from the RfL programme.

Chapter 11

Delivering the RfL Curriculum

The Readiness for Life (RfL) programme is extremely flexible and can be implemented with individual students, small groups or whole classes. Although the programme is curriculum-based, it has been designed to engage students on a more personal and reflective level to feel less like an ordinary lesson.

The way in which a facilitator engages students and delivers each RfL session is extremely important, particularly when working with hard-to-reach youth and those already at risk of disengaging from education. It is suggested that facilitators always begin and end an RfL session in the same way.

Starting an RfL session

Space allowing, gather everyone in a seated circle, including yourself, and start an introductory go-round in each session. This process helps everyone to become present in the room, leaving behind conversations and interactions with others, and also helps participants to get to know one another. Even though young people may have been in the same school or class for many years, they may know very little about one another! Circle processes help to break down barriers and build relationships.

- The facilitator should always go first to model the process.

- Use a 'talking object' if needed – a small object such as a ball which signifies who should be able to speak at any given time. If a person is holding the talking object they have the space to speak while others listen. No one should interrupt unless they are holding the talking object, which they can request by raising their hand.

- Encourage participants to use one another's names and address people directly by looking them in the eye. The circle processes should develop students' prosocial skills.

- Create equanimity in the circle by ensuring everyone is involved and is seated at the same height.

You may wish to begin the go-round by asking students to complete one of the following sentences – this will be particularly useful at the start of the programme if students don't know each other very well. For example:

- 'My name is…and something I enjoy doing in my spare time is…'
- 'My name is…and something fun I did this weekend was…'
- 'My name is…and my best memory is…'
- 'My name is…and if I could be someone else for a day I would be…'

Each student should repeat the same sentence, with the facilitator modelling the process initially.

You may also wish to introduce some short games and ice-breakers at the start of each session, particularly at the beginning of RfL. This can help to diffuse any tension or anxiety about participating in a new programme, build relationships, and start on a fun, lighter note.

Setting the tone

Maintaining appropriate conduct and behaviour is important in an RfL session, as it would be in any classroom. Creating boundaries will keep everyone physically and emotionally safe, and allow students to explore new concepts and ideas, build their confidence and self-esteem and not feel afraid to try new skills, which is crucial when aiming to raise aspirations and motivate youth to succeed.

Creating a safe, welcoming space is particularly important for young people at risk of disengaging from education, who may perceive school to be a hostile environment. There are a number of ways to create a welcoming space, particularly when working with small groups. For instance:

- Be consistent: try to hold RfL sessions on the same day and at the same time each week.

- Dedicate a specific room for RfL sessions that isn't used by other staff and students, to create a sense of privacy.

- Avoid introducing new students after the RfL programme has begun. Bringing a new young person into the programme halfway through can disrupt group cohesion, not to mention make it difficult for the incomer to feel included.

- Provide refreshments each session or on occasion: young people very much appreciate being able to help themselves to a hot drink or snack as they work and this helps sessions to feel less like a regular class. It also helps students to feel as though they're participating in the programme as a privilege, rather than it being another chore or compulsory punishment for poor behaviour or low academic scores.

- Gather students around one large table to do activities, or in small groups, and sit with students, rather than lecturing from the front of the room.

- Consider implementing a reward system for young people who demonstrate good behaviour or positive engagement, but be aware that solely using external rewards isn't enough to promote engagement.

- Use specific, positive praise often, to let students know they are doing well. Avoid generic praise such as 'great job' as this doesn't help a student to know what they did well and repeat the behaviour. Some students will rarely receive praise and it's vital for their self-worth and self-esteem.

- Break up sessions with games and short team-building activities to keep the energy high and participants engaged.

Keeping promises

Young people participating in an RfL session should be aware that the same rules for behaviour and conduct apply as they would in any other class or programme. Having a copy of the school rules can be useful, to direct students' attention as needed.

It can be beneficial to create your own rules or 'promises' that specifically apply to RfL sessions when working with small groups of students. Creating shared rules promotes ownership and responsibility for maintaining appropriate conduct. Referring to rules as 'promises' is less authoritarian and can help students to understand the behaviours they *should* exhibit, rather than those they *shouldn't*. Promises should be created by everyone, ideally in the first RfL session.

- Work as a group to identify promises for when you're participating in an RfL session.

- Encourage students to identify promises for behaviour, engagement, their interactions with others, etc.

- Stress that these promises are for everyone, including you as the facilitator.

- Write the promises on a large sheet of paper.

- Strive to reach a consensus for each promise that is to be recorded.

- Phrase each promise positively, e.g. instead of 'Don't talk over other people' suggest 'Listen to the person who is meant to be speaking'.

- Ask students to identify any promises for you as the facilitator – even though all promises apply to the whole group, they typically enjoy this idea!

- Don't list too many – six to eight promises are enough.

- Ask everyone to sign their agreement to the promises on the sheet and display it somewhere prominent.

- Refer back to the promise sheet as and when you need to. It should be displayed somewhere prominent in each RfL session.

Ending each RfL session

Just as each RfL session should start the same way, with an opening circle go-round and a reminder of group promises, it is suggested that each session end in the same way also, bringing students back to a circle and taking a few minutes to reflect upon the theme of the session and the learning or insights gained. You may also wish to share your own reflections and praise for students' development.

You may wish to ask each student to share one thing they have learned in the session or will take away with them, or to share a reflection about someone else in the group, e.g. 'I noticed Steven was listening really well today' or 'I think Ellen gave a good presentation.' This may be difficult for students initially, but should become easier as they relax into the process, build relationships and learn the language and process of reflection.

Managing behaviour issues

Poor behaviour should not be tolerated in an RfL session, just as it would not be accepted in any other class or programme. Students who consistently misbehave or disrupt the sessions should be excluded from participating after they have received fair warning, but avoid this as much as possible, as typically these students need the programme most of all! Other suggestions for managing poor behaviour include:

- Consistently notice students who are behaving well and reflect their actions to the rest of the group – praise and positive recognition is very important for young people, and students need to know how they *should* be behaving.

- Refer students to class or school rules.

- Refer students displaying inappropriate behaviour to the promises sheet and remind them of their commitment to behave appropriately.

- Explain why their behaviour is inappropriate to creating a learning opportunity.

Ending the RfL programme

The RfL programme is extremely flexible: the curriculum can be utilised for ad hoc lessons, can be delivered over a fixed period of time with individuals or groups, or the full programme can be delivered over weekly, hourly sessions for a full academic year to a group of identified young people.

As a long-term initiative the RfL programme will likely create strong bonds between participants and a sense of group cohesion that may make ending difficult for some. There will hopefully be a sense of achievement for students and pride in their progress, but also sadness at finishing and a loss of the group and the process. Managing endings is an important part of running a programme.

Here are some tips for ending an RfL programme:

- Prepare students for ending: they should be aware of how many weeks or sessions they have left.

- Ensure students complete the RfL questionnaire before you end, so you can measure success and progress.

- Plan a celebration event and engage students in the planning.

- Recognise each student's efforts, learning and progress – each person will take something different away from the programme, but it is important to recognise the time, commitment and effort each person has given.

- Distribute student certificates to recognise their engagement in the programme. A certificate template is included in Appendix 2.

- Encourage students to reflect upon their own progress over the course of the programme and to highlight their achievements.

- Activities to draw the programme to a close are contained in *Theme 8: Ignition*.

Chapter 12

Monitoring and Evaluation

Measuring the impact of any new programme or initiative is always important: you may wish to assess the value for money or the impact upon students' academic scores, or track improvements to the wider school culture and ethos. There are many benefits to introducing the Readiness for Life (RfL) programme to your school or setting, not only for the individual students participating in the programme, but for their peers, teaching staff and the wider community. The more engaged students are in their education the less likely they are to demonstrate anti-social and risk-taking behaviours, commit crimes or abuse illegal substances.

Assessing young people's needs and measuring success

The RfL programme includes a questionnaire to identify young people's attitudes and needs as they enter the programme, and measure the success of RfL upon completion. The questionnaire will help to measure students':

- aspirations for the future
- attitudes to school and further education
- perceptions of their soft skills, attributes and abilities.

You can also break down the questionnaire results by age of student, gender and ethnicity to look for trends.

It is recommended that each student complete the RfL questionnaire (found in Appendix 1) in the first RfL session, and towards the very end of the programme. You may also wish to ask students to complete the questionnaire midway through the programme to target resources and organise the curriculum in response to students' needs or gaps in knowledge highlighted in the questionnaire results.

Schools introducing a shorter or less intensive version of the programme should also use the questionnaire to demonstrate the programme's impact. You may also wish to track other indicators of the programme's success against a control group of non-participating students, including:

MONITORING AND EVALUATION

- school attendance of participating students
- academic attainment
- incidents of poor behaviour
- instances of truancy
- destinations of young people post-programme (if the programme culminates at the end of their school experience, or this data can be tracked over time).

Part III

The Readiness for Life (RfL) Curriculum

Theme 1

Believing in Me

Believing in Me builds a strong foundation on which young people will explore their future success and develop positive aspirations. Young people will explore their inner strengths and talents, building the positive attitudes and beliefs they will need for the future.

Learning objectives

By the end of this module, students will:

- understand the link between their thoughts, feelings and behaviours
- understand the concept of beliefs and identify their own beliefs about themselves and the world
- explore how their beliefs and values impact upon their day-to-day behaviour
- begin to explore their thoughts, ideas and beliefs about work, the future and success
- begin to identify their strengths and skills that can support positive aspirations.

Activities

- The Recipe for Success
- Getting to Know Me
- My Life Map
- Locus of Control
- Needs, Success and Aspirations
- Core Beliefs
- Self-Belief.

THEME 1: BELIEVING IN ME

Activity 1: Recipe for Success
BELIEVING IN ME

Learning objectives	To define and understand the concept of success
	To explore the difference between universal or stereotypical ideas of success and personal measures of success
	To identify stereotypes and assumptions about success
	To begin to define students' own ideas about success, and the skills and competencies they already possess to create personal success
Resources required	Large sheets of paper; marker pens

SET THE SCENE

Explore with students the idea that there is no one clear definition of success. It is a personal measure, and is unique to all of us. Some cultures have certain ideas about success which can lead people to think that there is only one way to be successful; for example, in Western countries we consider successful people to be those who work long hours and earn high wages. In other cultures success might be viewed differently.

EXPLORE

Above all, it is important for each person to think about their own life and what makes them feel successful. Discuss with students what it feels like to be successful. How do you feel inside when you have done something you are proud of or you have reached an achievement?

Give each student a large sheet of paper and marker pens and ask them to consider what might be their own personal ingredients for success. For example:

- their strengths and talents
- the skills they have
- aspects of their personality and character.

Each young person should create a poster to show their recipe for success. When ready, ask each student to present their poster and share how these ingredients have helped them to be a success already. What have they achieved so far in their life? (Note: if students struggle to identify any personal successes ask the group to contribute, or suggest some of the student's successes yourself if you know the student well enough).

ACTIVITY 1: RECIPE FOR SUCCESS

TAKE IT FORWARD

To conclude the lesson, discuss the following points:

- Can you be successful in one part of your life but not in other parts? e.g. successful at work but not at home? What might this look like?

- What does success now mean to you?

- What is one way in which you would like to be successful in your life?

EXTENSION ACTIVITY

Ask students to find three examples of people they consider to be successful, and bring a photograph or some information about each person to the next RfL session. These might be people the young person knows, such as family or friends, a celebrity or public figure, or someone they have read about in a book or magazine. Ask each student to share their three examples and to provide some details about why they consider those people to be successful.

THEME 1: BELIEVING IN ME

Activity 2: Getting to Know Me
BELIEVING IN ME

> **Learning objectives** To encourage students to explore their personal history and the link between their past, present and potential future outcomes
> To explore the link between self-perceptions and behaviours
> To build awareness of each individual's power to control their future
> To begin to develop positive aspirations and goals for the future
>
> **Resources required** Marker pens; Resource 1.1: Outline of a Person

SET THE SCENE

Ask students to share any reflections or thoughts from the previous RfL activity. Has anyone's thoughts about success changed since that session?

Share with students the focus for this activity: exploring our personal history that has led us to where we are today. Ask students to discuss:

- What makes you who you are? (e.g. your characteristics, personality, cultural heritage, etc.)
- What parts of you will always remain the same?
- What parts of you can be changed?
- How might you go about changing parts of you, e.g. becoming a confident person instead of someone who is very shy?

EXPLORE

Give each student a copy of *Resource 1.1: Outline of a Person* and some marker pens. Each student should work individually to fill the outline of their person with words to describe themselves. This may include words to describe their personality, character, skills and attributes, culture and heritage, ethnicity, gender, religion, family, looks and other descriptors.

Next, around the outside of the person outline, each student should write words to describe how they think other people might see them. They should consider how their parents, friends, teachers, family members and so on might describe them.

ACTIVITY 2: GETTING TO KNOW ME

TAKE IT FORWARD

Come back together as a whole group and ask each student to share their work, if they feel comfortable doing so. Discuss:

- Are there any differences between how we describe ourselves and how we think others might describe us?
- Are these positive or negative differences?
- How would you like people to describe you?

THEME 1: BELIEVING IN ME

Activity 3: My Life Map
BELIEVING IN ME

Learning objectives	To define and understand our past and how it relates to our future
	To begin to create a vision for the future
	To explore the aspects of our lives that are positive and those that may be holding us back
Resources required	Large rolls of paper; marker pens; Resource 1.2: Ideal Me

SET THE SCENE

Explain to students that they will be creating a life map to help them identify where they are, where they've been and where they might be going in life. Ask students to share some ideas about what a life map might include or look like.

EXPLORE

Give each student a long sheet of paper – rolls of paper are ideal for this exercise – and a marker pen. Each student will create a visual map of their life, using a line to represent their life starting from birth and stretching into the future. There are no right or wrong ways to complete this exercise, and students can use words, images, or a combination of both to describe major milestones and life events that occurred in their past that helped to shape who they are now in the present. These milestones might be positive or negative, and should be added along their timeline using words, drawings or both.

Next, ask students to identify key milestones in their lives and add a word or description about themselves at that time, e.g. 'starting school – I was shy' or 'passed my piano exam – confident'.

Once they reach the present day they should continue their timeline into the future, adding ideas for milestones they hope will occur; for example, going to college or university, getting a job, getting married or having children.

Students can share their life map when complete, or choose to keep it private. Discuss:

- How have those major milestones affected you and the direction of your life?

- Can we choose how life events affect us and what happens to us in the future?

- How can our thoughts and actions help us to achieve our goals?

- Who has influenced your life?

- How can we use negative life events to positively push us forward and help us reach our goals?

Ask students to review their work again, and this time consider which words or descriptions they would like to change about themselves. In an ideal world, who would they like to be?

Hand out copies of *Resource 1.2: Ideal Me* to each student. Students should consider the four parts of their life listed in each circle on the worksheet – at home; at school; with my friends; and in the future. They should fill each circle with a description of their ideal self, e.g. how might they describe themselves at school in an ideal world? They might be hardworking, popular, successful, etc.

TAKE IT FORWARD

When complete, ask students to come back together as a whole group and share their findings and reflections. Discuss:

- How different is the ideal 'you' from the current 'you'?

- Who is in control of whether or not you can become the ideal you?

- What might need to change in your life to start you on a journey to success?

THEME 1: BELIEVING IN ME

Activity 4: Locus of Control
BELIEVING IN ME

> **Learning objectives** *To define and understand the concept of personal power, control and choice*
>
> *To explore the impact of internal and external control on our thoughts, feelings and actions*
>
> **Resources required** *Large sheets of paper and/or whiteboard; marker pens; Resource 1.3: Locus of Control*

SET THE SCENE

Write the words 'Locus of Control' on the whiteboard or display on a large sheet of paper. Ask students if anyone knows what this phrase might mean. Offer the following definition:

A person's locus of control is a phrase which means how much people believe that they can control events that affect them. A person's 'locus' can either be internal (the person believes they can control their life) or external (meaning they believe that their decisions and life are controlled by factors which they cannot influence, or by chance or fate). In short, this can be described as:

Internal Locus of Control: You make things happen

versus

External Locus of Control: Things happen to you

A person who feels powerless to control their life and destiny can be locked in an external locus of control way of thinking, whereby they feel as though they are at the mercy of chance. They might describe themselves as unlucky, or treated unfairly by the world as things just 'happen to them'.

Discuss:

- How might a person with external locus of control react when they fail an exam or school project? Why?

- How might a person with internal locus of control react if they failed an exam or project?

- What is the main difference between these two people? (i.e. the way they explain life to themselves; their thought processes and perceptions)

- What are the consequences of thinking that things happen to you, as opposed to thinking you can make things happen?

ACTIVITY 4: LOCUS OF CONTROL

EXPLORE

In groups of four to six people, ask students to draw an outline of a person on a large sheet of paper. Give each group either 'internal' or 'external' locus of control and ask them to describe the person they have drawn, and brainstorm ideas for the consequences of their thinking.

Come back together as a whole group and share thoughts and ideas from each group. Discuss:

- Which is the more positive person?
- Which person is more likely to be happy and successful in life? Why?
- Which person are you?

Pair students and give each pair a copy of *Resource 1.3: Locus of Control* worksheet. Each group should work together to read the examples and decide whether the person has an internal or external locus of control.

Come back together and discuss whether those statements are internal/external. What are the consequences of those types of thinking?

TAKE IT FORWARD

To conclude the lesson, discuss the following points:

- How do my thoughts influence how successful I am in life and the direction of my future?
- How can I begin to change my locus of control from external to internal (i.e. thinking 'things happen to me' to thinking 'I make things happen')?
- What is one NEW THOUGHT I can think this week which will help me to have more control in my life and to feel more empowered?

THEME 1: BELIEVING IN ME

Activity 5: Needs, Success and Aspirations
BELIEVING IN ME

Learning objectives	*To explore the concept of physical, social and emotional needs*
	To define and understand how our needs can drive our behaviour
	To explore the social and emotional needs we may have on a daily basis and how they influence thinking and behaviour
Resources required	*Copies of Resource 1.4: Needs Triangle*

SET THE SCENE

Ask students to share some examples of things we need on a daily basis. What is an example of a physical need? An emotional need? A social need?

Can anyone think of an emotional need they have had today? How did you meet that need?

Ask students to suggest why they think needs are important. All actions and behaviours we have are efforts to meet our needs. Sometimes we are aware of this, such as eating when we are hungry and in need of food. Sometimes we are not aware of the fact that we are acting a certain way to meet a need, such as showing off to meet our need for attention.

EXPLORE

Ask students to work individually to complete *Resource 1.4: Needs Triangle* worksheet. Students should spend ten minutes or so considering each part of the triangle and writing in examples of needs they have on a daily basis, regularly, and occasional needs. Around the triangle they should write examples of ways they go about meeting these needs.

Ask students to circle a few of their top needs – those that will help them to be happy and successful in life, both now and in the future.

Share responses as a whole group and discuss ideas for how we can meet our needs to help us reach our goals at school and in the future.

ACTIVITY 5: NEEDS, SUCCESS AND ASPIRATIONS

TAKE IT FORWARD
- -
Discuss:

- How can we meet our needs?

- Being able to meet our own needs is very important, as when we look to one person to give us everything we need we can end up relying on them too much and become a burden, or if for any reason that person is no longer in our life, we can feel lost and needy. How can you meet your top needs each day?

- Think of someone you really admire. What might be their top needs to help them to be happy and successful? How might they go about meeting those needs?

THEME 1: BELIEVING IN ME

Activity 6: Core Beliefs
BELIEVING IN ME

Learning objectives	*To explore the concept of core beliefs*
	To define and understand how our beliefs influence our thoughts and behaviours
	To explore the impact of positive and negative beliefs
	To encourage students to explore and define more empowering and positive beliefs
Resources required	*Resource 1.5: Belief Labels, cut into individual rectangles; Resource 1.6: My Beliefs*

SET THE SCENE

Ask students to share what they think a 'belief' is. What does it mean to hold a belief in something? Can anyone suggest some examples of beliefs?

Our core beliefs are usually formed in childhood and we consider them to be 100 per cent true. If someone believes something to be true and has done for many years, it can be very difficult to change their mind! Some of our beliefs may be positive, such as believing people to be friendly and helpful on the whole, and some may be more negative, such as believing that people might be out to get us, or that the world isn't a very safe place.

EXPLORE

Gather in a circle and place the belief labels found in *Resource 1.5* in the middle. Ask each student to spend a few moments looking over the labels, and when they are ready they should choose one belief that rings true for them, either selecting the label or just remembering their choice to allow for others to choose the same belief.

Ask each person in turn to read aloud their belief. When everyone has shared, discuss how it feels to hold that belief. How does that belief impact upon your life?

Give each student a copy of *Resource 1.6: My Beliefs* worksheet. They should consider each section and list some ideas for beliefs they hold about themselves, about school, and about their future.

ACTIVITY 6: CORE BELIEFS

TAKE IT FORWARD

Come back together as a whole group and discuss the following points:

- Are your beliefs mostly empowering and positive, or disempowering and negative? i.e. will these thoughts help you to be successful and in control of your future?

- How do your beliefs influence your behaviour and choices?

- What might happen if we continue to think and act upon negative beliefs?

- How can we change our beliefs?

- Can anyone think of examples of different beliefs you could hold that are more empowering?

THEME 1: BELIEVING IN ME

Activity 7: Self-Belief
BELIEVING IN ME

Learning objectives	To explore the concept of self-belief
	To define and understand how positive self-belief can empower people to take positive action, develop healthy relationships and feel happy
	To encourage students to identify positive self statements
Resources required	Large sheet of paper; marker pens; Resource 1.7: I'm Proud of Me

SET THE SCENE

Ask students to share some ideas about what is 'self-belief'. What does it mean to believe in ourselves?

Ask students to share an example of a person they think has self-belief. This might be someone they know in real life or a celebrity, etc. How would you describe this person?

Discuss the difference between self-belief and beliefs about myself, and ask students to share some examples of each:

Self-belief: trusting in your positive qualities, having self-confidence and self-worth.

Beliefs about myself: ideas you believe to be true about yourself, which may be positive or negative.

EXPLORE

Ask students to consider the consequences of having self-belief. What happens when someone believes in themselves? (e.g. they might try hard at school; keep going when something gets tough; not let other people get them down, etc.) Highlight to students that even people with strong self-belief suffer setbacks and disappointments, but their self-belief can keep them going and helps to motivate them to try harder.

Ask students to share some ideas for what a person with self-belief might say to themselves, and what a person with little or no self-belief might say. How might those thoughts and words help a person to be successful, or to fail?

Ask students to work individually to complete *Resource 1.7: I'm Proud of Me* worksheet. They should spend a few minutes completing the sentence 'I am proud that I...' as many times as they can.

Come back together as a whole group and ask if anyone wants to share any reasons why they are proud. Discuss how it felt to complete the worksheet.

ACTIVITY 7: SELF-BELIEF

TAKE IT FORWARD

As a final activity tack a big sheet of paper on one wall with the sentence 'We have self-belief because...' written in the middle.

Ask students to graffiti the paper with as many ideas as they can think of to finish this sentence and display the sheet somewhere prominent in the classroom.

Resource 1.1
Outline of a Person

Resource 1.2
Ideal Me

Consider the four parts of your life in each circle below – at home; at school; with your friends; and in the future. Write or draw a description of your ideal self in each circle, e.g. how might you describe yourself at school in an ideal world? You might be hardworking, popular, successful, etc.

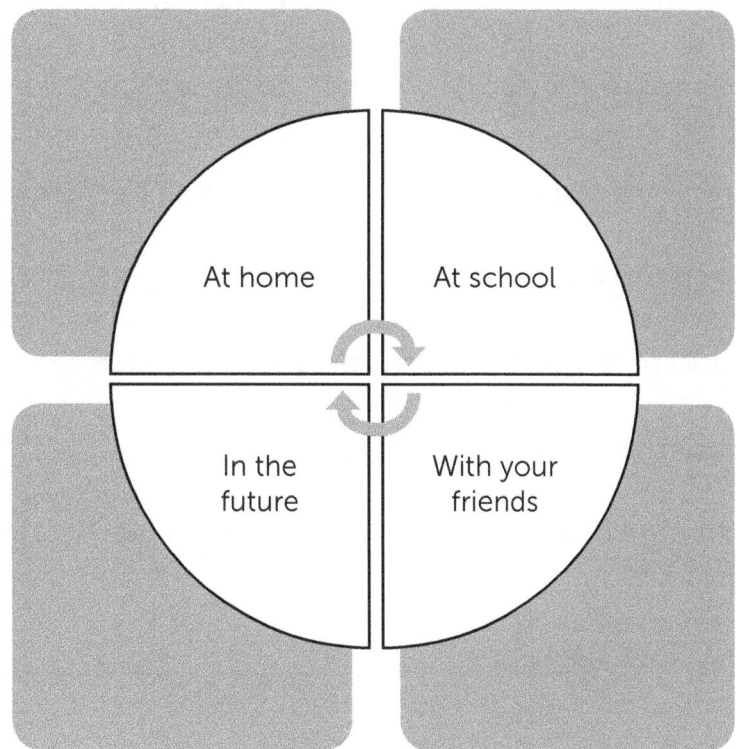

Which area of your life would you like to improve first?

What steps do you need to take to enable you to become this ideal you?

COPYRIGHT © NIKKI GIANT – *LIFE SKILLS AND CAREER COACHING FOR TEENS* – 2019

Resource 1.3
Locus of Control

A person's locus of control means how much people believe that they can control events that affect them.

Internal Locus of Control: You make things happen

versus

External Locus of Control: Things happen to you

Read the examples below and decide whether the person has an *internal* or *external* locus of control.

1. 'I failed my science test because the teacher didn't prepare us properly.'

    Internal or external locus of control? _____

2. 'I scored a goal in football because I practised so much.'

    Internal or external locus of control?_____

3. 'My mum shouted at me because I chose not to clean my room after she'd asked me to do it.'

    Internal or external locus of control? _____

4. 'It's so unfair that my dad grounded me for no reason, he just doesn't want me to have fun!'

    Internal or external locus of control? _____

5. 'I guess I just got lucky when I was picked for the hockey team.'

    Internal or external locus of control? _____

6. **'I got the job because I spent a long time on my application and asked people to help me.'**

   Internal or external locus of control? _____

7. **'Good things don't happen to people like me.'**

   Internal or external locus of control? _____

8. **'I am in control of my future, and I will go to university if I work hard.'**

   Internal or external locus of control? _____

Resource 1.4
Needs Triangle

Consider each part of the triangle and write in examples of physical, emotional and social needs you have on a daily basis, regularly, and occasional needs. Around the triangle write examples of ways you go about meeting these needs.

EXAMPLES
- -
Every day: sleep
Regular: time with friends
Occasional: independence

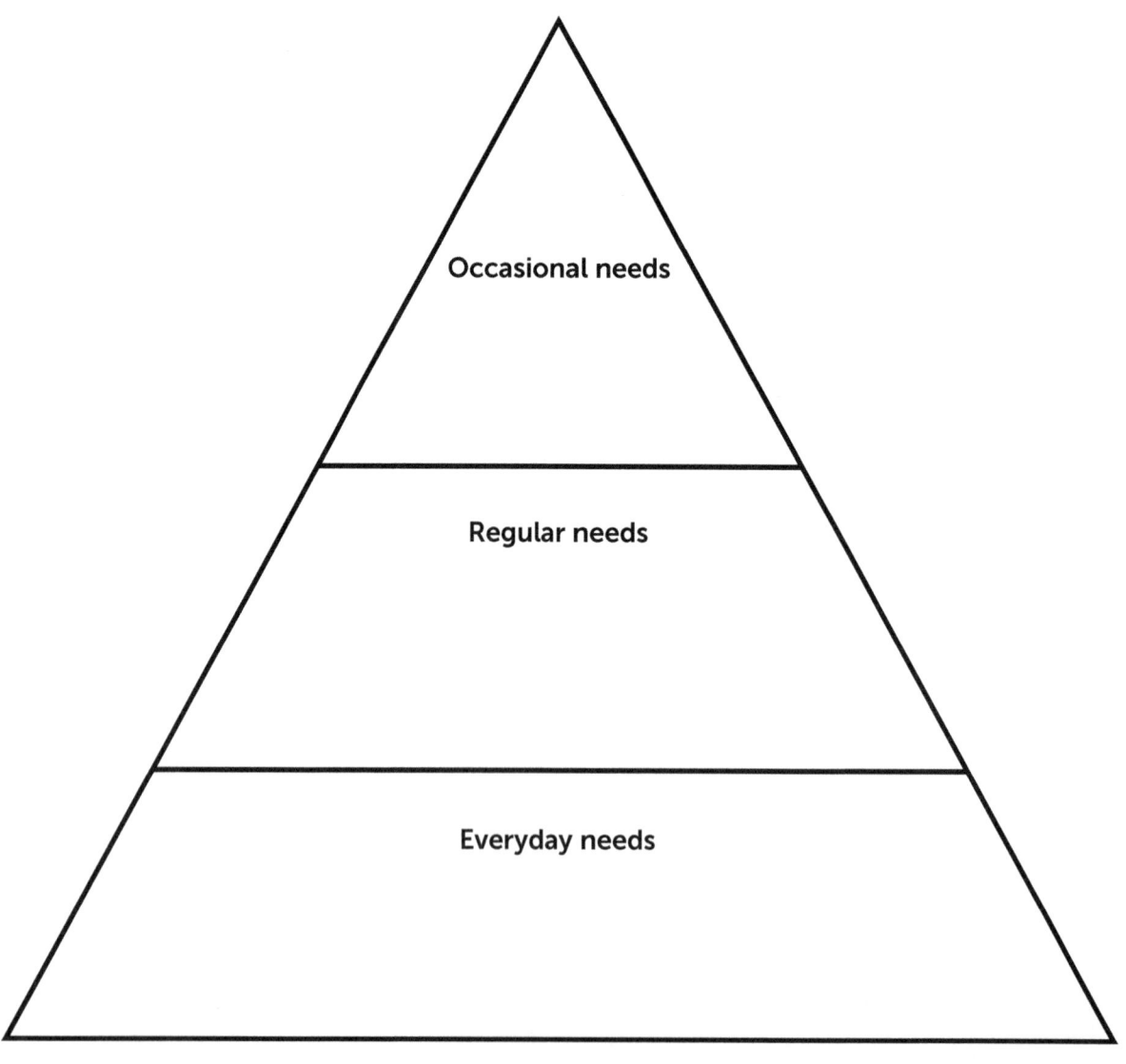

Resource 1.5
Belief Labels

I am worthy of good things	People want to be around me
I like being me	I am worthy of receiving good things in life
I am clever	I am capable
I am attractive	I am skilled and good at certain things
I am well liked by others	The future looks exciting

People are generally nice and kind	I am capable of dealing with anything that comes my way
My future is filled with fun and joy	I am positive and optimistic
I am on an adventure	I have a purpose in life
I am loved	Other people need me
I have unique gifts to share with the world	I am listened to and respected by others

Life is a struggle	I don't have anything unique to offer
I need to change who I am to fit in	I'm not capable of achieving the things that other people can
I am not worth as much as others	My future is set in stone
I am not good enough as I am	I am unconfident
I don't fit in at school	I am not wanted

People are dishonest and lie	People are out to get me
I am incapable of reaching my goals and dreams	There is nothing special about me
People like me don't achieve much	Success is all about luck
People can't be trusted	I give up easily
My thoughts and opinions don't matter	I don't have what it takes to be successful

Resource 1.6
My Beliefs

Our core beliefs are usually formed in childhood and in general we consider them to be accurate and true. Some of our beliefs may be positive, such as believing that people are generally friendly and helpful, and some may be negative, such as believing that people might be out to get us, or the world isn't a very safe place.

Consider your personal beliefs about yourself, about school, and about the future, and write some examples of things you believe to be true in each box.

Example: Beliefs about me – I believe I am a good person and I have many skills and talents.

Example: Beliefs about the future – I believe that I am not in control of my future. I believe people like me don't go to university or get good jobs.

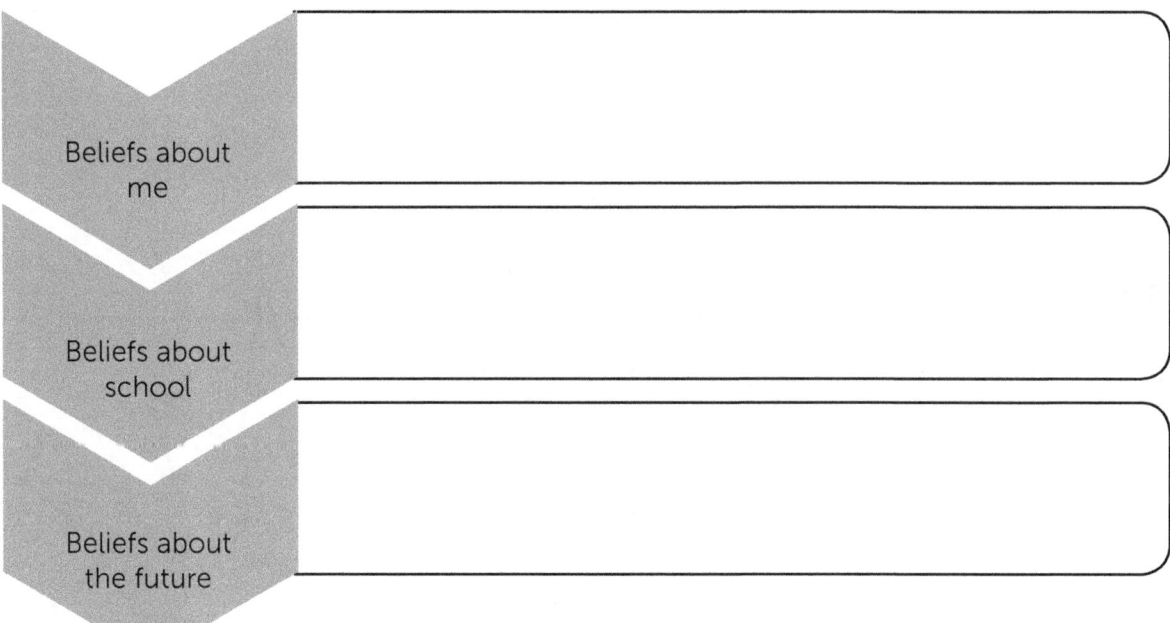

Which beliefs are serving you well and helping you to achieve your goals? Which are not?

Resource 1.7
I'm Proud of Me

It's important to acknowledge all of our strengths, skills, talents and accomplishments, and share them with others! Consider all of the many different reasons why you are proud to be you and write them in the spaces below.

I'm proud of myself because…

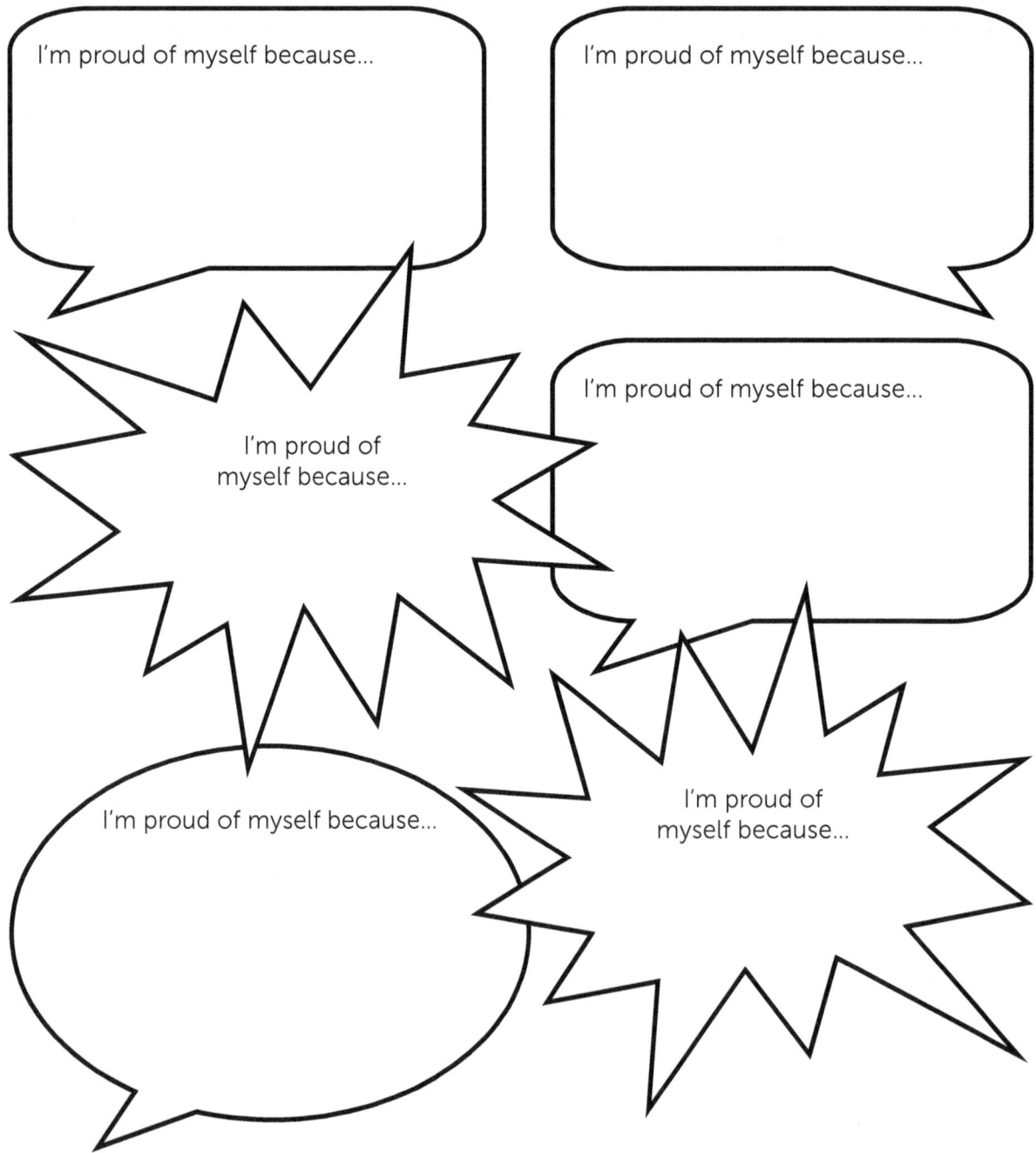

Theme 2

Skills for Life

Skills for Life explores the practical skills young people need to succeed in the workplace. Essential skills such as presenting to a group or working as a team are often not explicitly taught or modelled to youth, while crucial competencies such as critical thinking and using initiative are the preserve of the few, not the many. While most employers state that these are the most important qualities they seek in the next generation of workers, young people are left in the dark. Skills for Life helps youth to work together to explicitly explore and practise skills as diverse as networking and problem solving.

Learning objectives

By the end of this module, students will:

- acknowledge the range of interpersonal and practical skills needed in the workplace and identify the range of applications for such skills

- develop their ability to work with others as a team, developing team-working and collaboration skills

- develop confidence, public speaking and presentation skills to utilise in a range of settings

- practise interview skills to build confidence and language to use in interviews and formal meetings

- understand the purpose of networking and practise ways to network with others, developing social skills and relationships.

Activities

- Team Building
- Who's Right for the Job?
- Who Do You Need on Your Team?

THEME 2: SKILLS FOR LIFE

- Are You a Team Player?
- Problem Solving
- Networking
- Networking Skills
- Interview Skills
- Agree or Disagree?
- Presentation Skills
- First Impressions.

Activity 1: Team Building
SKILLS FOR LIFE

Learning objectives	*To explore the concept of working as a team*
	To define and practise team-working skills and explore their value
	To identify useful team-working skills and their applications
Resources required	*Marshmallows; a packet of spaghetti; large sheet of paper and/or whiteboard*

SET THE SCENE

Introduce the theme for this session: team building. Ask students to suggest some ideas about why teamwork is important at school and in the workplace. Why do we need to be a team player?

Explain to students that they will play some games with an emphasis on teamwork.

EXPLORE

Discuss:

- What skills and qualities do you need to be a team player?
- How might you demonstrate effective teamwork?

Record their answers on the whiteboard or on a large sheet of paper to refer back to.

Explain to students that they will play two games that will test their team-working skills. Split students into two groups, or groups of four to six people if you have a large number.

Human Knots

Spread out so each group has enough room to move and instruct each group to stand in a tight circle with their shoulders almost touching. Each person should reach into the centre of the circle and grab someone else's hand across the circle – each person must hold hands with two different people.

When everyone is ready, instruct each group to try to untangle the circle so everyone is holding hands regularly in a circle – when the circle is formed, some people can be facing out and some in. They cannot let go of one another's hands!

Discuss:

- What team-working skills did you use to help you in that game?
- What would you do differently next time? Why?

THEME 2: SKILLS FOR LIFE

Marshmallow Towers

Give each group four pieces of dried spaghetti and six large marshmallows. Instruct students to build the tallest tower possible in three minutes using only the spaghetti and marshmallows. They will need to get creative and use their engineering skills for this task! The tower must be able to stand on its own for 30 seconds once the time is up.

Discuss:

- What skills did you use this time?
- What would you do differently next time?
- Did you learn anything from the last game which helped you this time?

TAKE IT FORWARD

Discuss:

- Is being a team player more important than working well independently?
- Does someone need to be a leader when you're working as a team, or can each person be involved equally?
- What does it mean to lead a team? What skills does a leader need?
- Why is it important to be a team player in the workplace?
- Can anyone think of an example of a job that requires good team-working skills?
- Does every job require team-working skills?

Activity 2: Who's Right for the Job?
SKILLS FOR LIFE

Learning objectives *To identify the qualities an employer seeks in an employee*
To begin to explore our employability and identify skills required for a job
To identify our own skills and qualities that are attractive to an employer

Resources required *Resource 2.1: Potential Employee Case Studies; Resource 2.2: I'm the Boss*

SET THE SCENE

Ask students to suggest some examples of qualities they would look for in a potential employee if they were the boss and looking to hire someone. Highlight the importance of personal qualities and attributes in the workplace as well as practical skills and experience.

EXPLORE

In this activity the tables are turned and the students will be the boss with the power to hire and fire!

Split students into groups of four to six and give each group *Resource 2.1: Potential Employee* Case Studies and *Resource 2.2: I'm the Boss*.

Each group should read the selection of descriptions of potential employees. Next, students should read the scenario describing what the boss is looking for in an employee. Each group should make a note of any particular needs the boss has – what kind of skills, experience and personality might s/he be looking for?

The boss needs to hire two people from the list. The group must work together to decide which two people they would hire, and why.

TAKE IT FORWARD

Discuss:

- Which people did you decide to hire? Why?

- Which is more important – having the right skills for the job, or the right personality and personal qualities?

- How can you show a potential employer what skills and experience you have to offer?

- How can you show a potential employer what personal qualities you have to offer?

THEME 2: SKILLS FOR LIFE

Activity 3: Who Do You Need on Your Team?

SKILLS FOR LIFE

> **Learning objectives** *To explore the concept of a team*
> *To explore the ways in which people we trust can help us to reach our goals*
> *To identify the help we need from others*
>
> **Resources required** *Resource 2.3: Who Do You Need on Your Team?*

SET THE SCENE

Each of us needs our own 'team' in life, to help us reach our goals and manage difficult times. Our team might consist of our family, friends, teachers, youth worker, members of our church or other people we trust. However, having a team is only of use when we reach out to them and ask for their support.

EXPLORE

Using the worksheet in *Resource 2.3*, ask students to work individually to make a list of the people in their personal team. This list might include people they already have 'in their corner' or those they want to approach and ask for help. Next, students should consider how these 'team members' could help them, recording their answers on the worksheet.

TAKE IT FORWARD

Discuss:

- Why is it important to have a team around us?

- How can you reciprocate and provide help to your team? What might you be able to offer? Remember help and support should go two ways.

Activity 4: Are You a Team Player?

SKILLS FOR LIFE

> **Learning objectives** *To explore the concept of a team*
> *To identify the qualities of a team player*
> *To identify the importance of teamwork in the workplace*
>
> **Resources required** *Resource 2.4: Are You a Team Player?*

SET THE SCENE

Ask students to suggest some examples of ways in which they can be a team player. Why is it important to work together as a team?

EXPLORE

Distribute copies of the quiz *Are You a Team Player?* to each student (*Resource 2.4*). Students should work individually to answer the questions and score themselves accordingly. Ask each person to add up their scores and ask students to share their scores with the group if they feel comfortable doing so.

TAKE IT FORWARD

Discuss:

- Are you a good team player?

- Which team-working skills might you need to work on and strengthen?

- What is the opposite of being a good team player? How would you describe this person?

THEME 2: SKILLS FOR LIFE

Activity 5: Problem Solving
SKILLS FOR LIFE

Learning objectives	*To explore the skill of problem solving and identify its purpose*
	To practise problem solving
	To acknowledge the different methods and styles of solving problems
Resources required	*Resource 2.5: Problem Solving Case Studies; Resource 2.6: Problem Solvers Worksheet*

SET THE SCENE

Introduce the theme for this activity: problem solving.

Ask students to suggest why it is important that we are good problem solvers. How would this skill be useful in college or in the workplace?

The ability to solve problems and demonstrate critical thinking skills (analysing and evaluating things) is one of the top skills employers say they most want to see in young people.

EXPLORE

Ask students to read the case studies in *Resource 2.5* in small groups of four to six and use the prompts in *Resource 2.6* to solve the problem.

Ask each group to present their solutions.

TAKE IT FORWARD

Discuss:

- How do you usually solve problems? How effective is that method?
- Are there different ways to solve a problem?
- How could you show an employer that you're a problem solver?
- What words would you use to describe a problem solver?

Activity 6: Networking
SKILLS FOR LIFE

> **Learning objectives**
> *To explore the concept of networking*
> *To identify the value of networking*
> *To explore different methods of networking*
> *To identify people to network with to achieve our goals*
>
> **Resources required** *Resource 2.7: Networking Worksheet*

SET THE SCENE

Introduce the theme for this activity: networking. Ask students if they have heard of this term before, and what they think it means.

Share the following definition: networking is the process of building relationships and interacting with others to exchange information and develop contacts. Networking is particularly useful for people looking to develop their career.

EXPLORE

Discuss:

- What might networking look like?
- There are lots of different types of networking. Can anyone think of a way to network if you were looking for a job or volunteering opportunity?
- Who could you network with?

Provide students with some examples if they need them, e.g. networking with people you know, online using social media, at job fairs and careers events, by contacting organisations to ask for opportunities, etc.

Ask students to create a personal brainstorm using the worksheet in *Resource 2.7*. Students should write their dream job or job goal in the middle of the worksheet, and then fill in the boxes titled 'Who (What sort of person should I be networking with or who do I know that can help?)'; 'What (What do I need help with? What's the purpose of networking?)'; 'How (What are my next steps? How am I going to do this?)'; and 'Where (Where can I go for more help, advice or support?)'.

TAKE IT FORWARD

Ask students to share their networking brainstorms.
Discuss:

- How will you use your network?
- What's your favourite method of networking?

THEME 2: SKILLS FOR LIFE

Activity 7: Networking Skills
SKILLS FOR LIFE

> **Learning objectives** *To explore the concept of networking*
> *To define and explore the skills and personal qualities needed for networking*
> *To practise networking with peers*
>
> **Resources required** *Resource 2.8: Find Someone*

SET THE SCENE

You should ideally complete the previous exercise before introducing this activity, to ensure students understand the concept of networking.

Explain to students that this activity will focus on the skills they will need when networking, especially in formal, face-to-face situations, such as at a job fair.

EXPLORE

Remind students that networking is the process of meeting people, asking questions about their job, experience and skills, presenting the same information and finding the people who might be able to offer help, advice or a route to success.

Ask students to suggest some ideas for skills they might need to network. What kind of personal qualities might you need to be a good networker?

Distribute copies of *Resource 2.8: Find Someone* – one per person. Each student should network with their fellow students, writing their name in the first column and filling in the second and third columns with the students' skills, experience and dream job.

Students should practise the skills they need for successful networking, including asking questions, listening, and talking about themselves positively. When complete, ask students to review the sheet and see who they have the most in common with.

TAKE IT FORWARD

Discuss:

- If this were a real networking scenario, who would you choose to contact? Who might help you to get the sort of job you want?

- What are the main skills you used to help you network?

- How did it feel to talk about your skills, experience and dream job?

Activity 8: Interview Skills
SKILLS FOR LIFE

> **Learning objectives**   *To identify the skills and qualities needed to succeed at interviews*
> *To explore methods of preparing for an interview*
> *To identify positive actions to take before, during and after an interview*
>
> **Resources required**   *Large sheets of plain paper; marker pens*

SET THE SCENE

Introduce the theme for this activity: interview skills. People will go through many interviews in their lifetime, for volunteering roles, jobs, college and university and more. Interviews are very important processes to help both sides decide if they are right for one another.

Ask students to suggest what skills and personal qualities are needed for a successful interview.

EXPLORE

In groups of approximately four to six, ask students to draw two lines down a large sheet of paper, splitting the sheet into three sections. Students should work together to brainstorm what they would need to do before an interview, during an interview, and after an interview. For example:

Before: Print a copy of your CV; practise answering questions; choose a suitable, professional outfit to wear.

During: Ask questions; be polite.

After: Thank the interviewer; shake hands; follow up with a phone call or email.

Come back together as a whole group and share answers.

TAKE IT FORWARD

Discuss:

- Which interview skills might you need to improve?
- What might you find most difficult about being interviewed?

THEME 2: SKILLS FOR LIFE

Activity 9: Agree or Disagree?

SKILLS FOR LIFE

Learning objectives	*To explore ideas about interviews*
	To debate and discuss our personal values and beliefs
	To explore the helpful and unhelpful actions to take during an interview
	To encourage students to explore real-life scenarios related to employment and interviews
Resources required	*Resource 2.9: Agree–Disagree Labels*

SET THE SCENE

Ask students to recap on the skills and personal qualities needed to be effective during interviews.

EXPLORE

Explain to students that they will play a game to explore their views and opinions about interviews.

Tack the labels 'Agree' and 'Disagree' found in *Resource 2.9* on the walls at either end of the room, with the 'Don't Know' label on a wall in the middle.

Explain the rules of the game: the following statements will be read aloud and the group must decide whether they agree or disagree with the statement, or if they don't know. Students should 'vote with their feet' by going to stand next to the corresponding label.

Stress that there are no right or wrong answers, just their opinions. After each statement ask students to declare why they agree, disagree or don't know.

Scenarios

- You should try to present the best version of you in an interview, rather than be yourself.

- You shouldn't tell jokes during an interview.

- An interviewer will expect you to shake their hand when you begin and finish the interview.

- If you don't have the right skills for the job, you should lie and say you do during the interview – you can always learn on the job.

- It's OK to stretch the truth a little on your CV.

- If you know someone who works for the company, you should name-drop during the interview.
- You should take the job if it's offered to you, even if you felt a little uncomfortable with the interviewer and the role.

TAKE IT FORWARD

Discuss:

- What did you learn from this activity?
- Is there a right and wrong way to conduct an interview?
- What worries you the most about interviews? How can you address these worries now?

THEME 2: SKILLS FOR LIFE

Activity 10: Presentation Skills

SKILLS FOR LIFE

> **Learning objectives**   *To explore presentation skills*
> *To define and understand the methods of successful presentation*
> *To identify good and bad presentation skills*
> *To practise giving a presentation to peers in a safe environment*
>
> **Resources required**   *Large sheets of plain paper; marker pens*

SET THE SCENE

Introduce the theme of the session: presentation skills. Highlight to students the importance of being able to present ourselves, and our thoughts and ideas, when we attend interviews, have a job or volunteer position, or network professionally. Presentation skills are used in lots of different job roles, such as lawyers presenting their arguments, teachers presenting their lesson plans or designers presenting their drawings to clients.

Being a presenter doesn't come naturally to everyone, but it is a skill that can be learned.

EXPLORE

Ask students to suggest some examples of presentation skills. What do you need to do to effectively present yourself or your ideas? For example, speak clearly, speak loudly so everyone can hear, make eye contact with the audience, etc.

In groups of four to six, ask students to brainstorm some ideas for what a good presentation might look like, and what a bad presentation might involve, using a large sheet of paper and some marker pens. After a few minutes come back together as a whole group and share answers.

Next, ask students to get into pairs or threes. They must work together to create a sales presentation for a product or idea. They must imagine they are pitching a new product to the buying department of a large supermarket or shop. The rest of the group will be the 'buyers' and will watch the presentation and give constructive feedback.

Each group should decide upon their product (which can be new or existing) and plan their three-minute presentation. The presentation should include information about the product and why the supermarket should consider stocking it. Their general presentation style will also be considered. Each person in the group must take a turn to speak and present during their three-minute pitch.

ACTIVITY 10: PRESENTATION SKILLS

TAKE IT FORWARD

Ask students to share their thoughts about the presentations.
Discuss:

- How did you feel when you were presenting your product?
- Which presentation skills do you want to work on and improve?
- How can you become a better presenter?

THEME 2: SKILLS FOR LIFE

Activity 11: First Impressions
SKILLS FOR LIFE

Learning objectives *To explore the concept of creating a first impression*
To identify whether first impressions are important, and to explore ways to make a good first impression in general, in the workplace or at an interview
To explore the ways in which a successful person strives to make a good first impression

Resources required *Resource 2.10: First Impressions*

SET THE SCENE

Ask students to suggest why 'first impressions' matter when applying for college or a volunteer position, or in the workplace. Do first impressions really count?

We often form an impression of someone within seconds of meeting them – we decide whether a person is likeable or not, safe or a threat, whether we have much in common with them, and we even form impressions about their personality, such as deciding whether they are a confident person, or aggressive, or warm and open. Sometimes these judgements prove to be inaccurate and we form a new impression of the person, but other times our first impressions stick.

EXPLORE

Ask students to consider what first impression they make when they meet someone new for the first time.

Using the worksheet found in *Resource 2.10: First Impressions*, ask students to work individually and read the words listed, circling three to five that best describe the impression they think they make. Students should be as honest as they possibly can. They can also add their own ideas underneath if the word they need is not listed.

Next, each student should ask someone else in the group to choose three to five words they think best describe them and the impression they make.

ACTIVITY 11: FIRST IMPRESSIONS

TAKE IT FORWARD

Ask students to share their findings from the activity.
Discuss:

- Was anyone surprised when they started to think about the impression they make?

- Did anyone have a very different list of words when they asked someone to describe their first impression? How does this make you feel?

- Does anyone feel they want to change their first impression? How might you go about doing this?

- What creates a first impression? e.g. appearance; body language; facial expressions; how we introduce ourselves or interact with people, etc.

- How are presentation skills linked to first impressions?

- What kind of first impression does a successful person make?

Resource 2.1
Potential Employee Case Studies

POTENTIAL EMPLOYEE 1

Dan is 24 and has been working as a salesperson for a big IT firm in a large city. He joined the company with no experience but is now the top salesperson in the whole company, selling computer equipment to large offices and shops. He is used to dealing with IT technicians and managers of big companies who decide which IT equipment to buy. He describes himself as a 'go-getter' and is very ambitious. He doesn't like to report to anyone, preferring to work on his own. He describes his sales technique as cut-throat – making money is his primary objective and he's very good at it.

POTENTIAL EMPLOYEE 2

Dawn is 50 and works at a local care home for the elderly. She is a physical therapist, helping people to get back on their feet after a fall or illness. She has been doing this job for 20 years. She is used to working in a small team at the care home, and is not used to travelling with her work. She has never been a salesperson but would like to earn a bit more money than she does at the moment.

POTENTIAL EMPLOYEE 3

Chris is 35 and is currently unemployed. He was made redundant (let go) from his previous job two years ago and has struggled to find work ever since. He is a calm person and very sincere, and is very keen to get the job. He describes himself as a people-person, patient and loyal, and would like a long career with the same company. He has three small children at home and has been looking after them so his wife can work. He has a practical nature and a can-do attitude, being happy to pitch in and do what's needed.

POTENTIAL EMPLOYEE 4

Ali is 18 and has just finished college. He doesn't want to go to university yet and would like to take a job instead to earn some money. He is very good at using computers, is organised and did a business studies course in college, so he knows the basics of business management. He has been working part time in a shop as a salesperson. Ali was on the school debating team and is used to speaking in front of big groups of people. Ali describes himself as fun, sociable, enthusiastic and positive.

POTENTIAL EMPLOYEE 5

Sally is 30 and has been running her own business, selling handmade beauty products, for the last three years. She is struggling to cope with the stresses of working for herself and would like a more permanent job, so she can run her business on the side and not be reliant on it for money. Sally has experience of doing many different tasks associated with running a business, including selling, marketing, admin and keeping records, following up with customers and managing money. She has never worked with elderly people but she considers herself to be a good communicator.

Resource 2.2
I'm the Boss

Read the scenario below describing what the boss is looking for in an employee. You should consider any particular needs the boss has – what kind of skills, experience and personality might she or he be looking for?

> You are the boss of a small company, Disability Solutions Limited, that manufactures and sells equipment to help people who have mobility problems to get around more easily and stay in their own homes after an accident or illness. Some of your products include walking frames to help people who aren't very mobile, wheelchairs, and handrails to help people get in and out of the shower.
>
> Disability Solutions Limited is a family-owned company, set up five years ago. Since then it has grown from just three employees to forty, with staff manufacturing the items, managing the office, and organising sales.
>
> You need two new salespeople to join your team. The candidate will sell products directly to people who need them, over the phone and in person, plus selling in bulk to shops and other outlets.
>
> The new salespeople will be based at the office, but will spend a lot of time out and about, meeting customers, shopkeepers, and other clients. You need to be able to trust the people you hire, as they will be working independently quite often.
>
> Some of your customers are extremely ill, elderly and vulnerable. Your salespeople need to be able to communicate effectively, and be patient and kind, with good listening skills.
>
> The new salespeople will need to communicate with the manufacturing team to place the orders, and with the administration team in the office who will bill the customers. The salespeople will need to keep a log of all their sales and the profit they've made, keep track of their customers so they know when to contact them in the future with new products or for maintenance of their items, and be able to create and deliver presentations to big hospitals and large shops to persuade them to buy in bulk.

Consider:

- What skills and qualities do the salespeople need?
- What's most important?
- What skills or qualities can be taught or developed on the job?

The boss needs to hire two people from the list found in *Resource 2.1: Potential Employee Case Studies*. Decide which two people you would hire, and why.

Resource 2.3
Who Do You Need on Your Team?

Consider all of the people that are on your 'team' in life. These are the people who care about you, support you, and can help you in some way. This list might include people you already have 'in your corner' or those you want to approach and ask for help.

1.

2.

3.

4.

5.

6.

7.

8.

9.

10.

HOW CAN YOUR TEAM HELP YOU?

Name of person	What can they help you with?	Examples of situations they can help you with
e.g. Uncle Mark	He's good at writing. He works at the university.	CV writing. Visiting the university to see if it's right for me.

Resource 2.4
Are You a Team Player?

Read the following questions and decide if they apply to you or not. Add up your score at the end to see how good your team skills are.

1. **Your teacher has asked you to do a group project and deliver a presentation on Monday. On Sunday night you find out that someone hasn't done their work. What do you do?**

    a) Complete their part so you will all still receive a good grade.

    b) Pretend you didn't know and see what happens tomorrow.

    c) Contact the other team members to discuss the best thing to do.

2. **You play football for a local team and at the end of practice it starts raining. All of the other players disappear to get changed, leaving the coach to clear away all of the footballs, cones and goals on his own. What do you do?**

    a) Quickly go and help him without being asked – two people will be quicker than one.

    b) Pretend you didn't notice and slink off with the others.

    c) Look around to see if anyone else is left behind to see whether they will help first.

3. **Your friend asks you to help them revise for an exam at the weekend, but you've been invited to a party. What do you do?**

    a) Ditch the party and make sure you get your friend through their revision.

    b) Ignore their texts and make an excuse when you see your friend afterwards.

    c) Say nothing to your friend, but see if you can find someone else to help them, or casually suggest they're better off revising alone.

4. **You're working on a group project and everyone keeps shouting over one other, trying to get their point across. It's turning into a big argument and people are getting upset that they're not being listened to. What do you do?**

    a) Take the lead and ask everyone to calm down, and suggest each person takes their turn to speak.

    b) Walk off – it's pointless staying as nothing is being achieved.

    c) Get your phone out and play a game until everyone stops shouting.

5. **Your parents have gone out for the afternoon and left you in charge of your younger brother. He starts messing about and accidentally trips and falls, smashing your mum's favourite vase full of water and flowers. What do you do?**

    a) Tidy up the smashed pieces and clean up the mess before your parents come home and calmly tell them what happened.

    b) Leave your brother to clean up the mess and to confess to your parents.

    c) Help your brother tidy up the mess but disappear into your bedroom when your parents get home.

6. **One of your classmates has been very ill in hospital for a long time, and your group of friends have decided to throw her a party when she comes back to school. There are a lot of jobs to be done before the party and half the group have disappeared. What do you do?**

    a) Make a list of jobs that need to be done, call some other friends to help and stay behind late to make sure everything is ready.

    b) Go home – everyone else has, so why should you stay late? Someone else will do the jobs before the party.

    c) Call your friends to come back and help. If they don't, at least you tried.

What did you score?

Mostly As: You are an excellent team player! You think of others and strive to make sure you consider what's most important, rather than doing what's best for you. Be careful not to take on too much, though, as you might end up becoming resentful.

Mostly Bs: Team playing doesn't necessarily come naturally to you, but that's OK – try and take small steps to think about how you can support your friends and family. People will be there for you when you need them if they know they can rely on you, too.

Mostly Cs: You are able to be a team player and demonstrate good skills when it suits you, but sometimes your own needs can take over. Think about the small ways you can work with others to achieve your goals.

Resource 2.5
Problem Solving Case Studies

You are working in a group with four friends on a school project. You have been asked to give a presentation about an idea for a business you have been working on for the last three weeks. The presentation counts for 50 per cent of your final grade. When you get to the classroom to present to your teachers, the PowerPoint you've prepared won't work. The slides won't display and everyone is waiting for you to start.

You are looking for a part-time job and someone suggested you hand out copies of your CV to different shops or restaurants that might be looking for part-time workers. You go into one of your favourite stores and the assistant tells you that they are actually looking to hire someone. The manager comes to speak to you and asks if you would come in for an interview right now. You weren't prepared for this, and now you're panicking!

You've spent the last six weeks revising for a history exam as it's your least favourite subject and you often struggle with it. You focused on preparing answers for questions about World War 2 as you thought the exam would only be on this topic, but when you get into the exam hall and open the paper you see that all of the questions are about a completely different theme that you haven't revised much at all.

You have a part-time job helping out at a restaurant. You've become quite close with someone else who works with you, and would consider them a friend. The manager is quite bossy and can be aggressive at times. One day your friend texts you to say they've overslept and asks you to lie for them, telling the boss that they're ill.

You really want to apply for a college course to study something you love, but you're not very good at writing and the application is really long. You tell your mum you've already done it to get her off your back, but in reality you keep putting it off until it's the day before the deadline. You have to get it done tonight or you won't be able to go to college and you'll have to confess to your mum, but you just don't know where to start.

Resource 2.6
Problem Solvers Worksheet

Using the case studies in *Resource 2.5*, identify the main problems and list the possible solutions or courses of action you could take, and analyse the pros and cons of that solution.

Identify the problem	Possible solution or course of action	Pros and cons of the solution
e.g. struggling to understand maths problems	Ask a friend to show you. Ask your teacher for an extra class. Get a book out of the library.	+ Friend can help quickly. - They might have misunderstood the problem too.

Resource 2.7
Networking Worksheet

Networking is the process of building relationships and interacting with others to exchange information and make contact with new people who can offer us help, advice or support. Networking is particularly useful when you're looking for a job or voluntary position – people often say, 'It's not what you know, it's who you know,' and networking can help. Consider your dream job or a career-related goal. Think about who you might need to network with to help you achieve that goal, how, what you need from them, and where you could go for support.

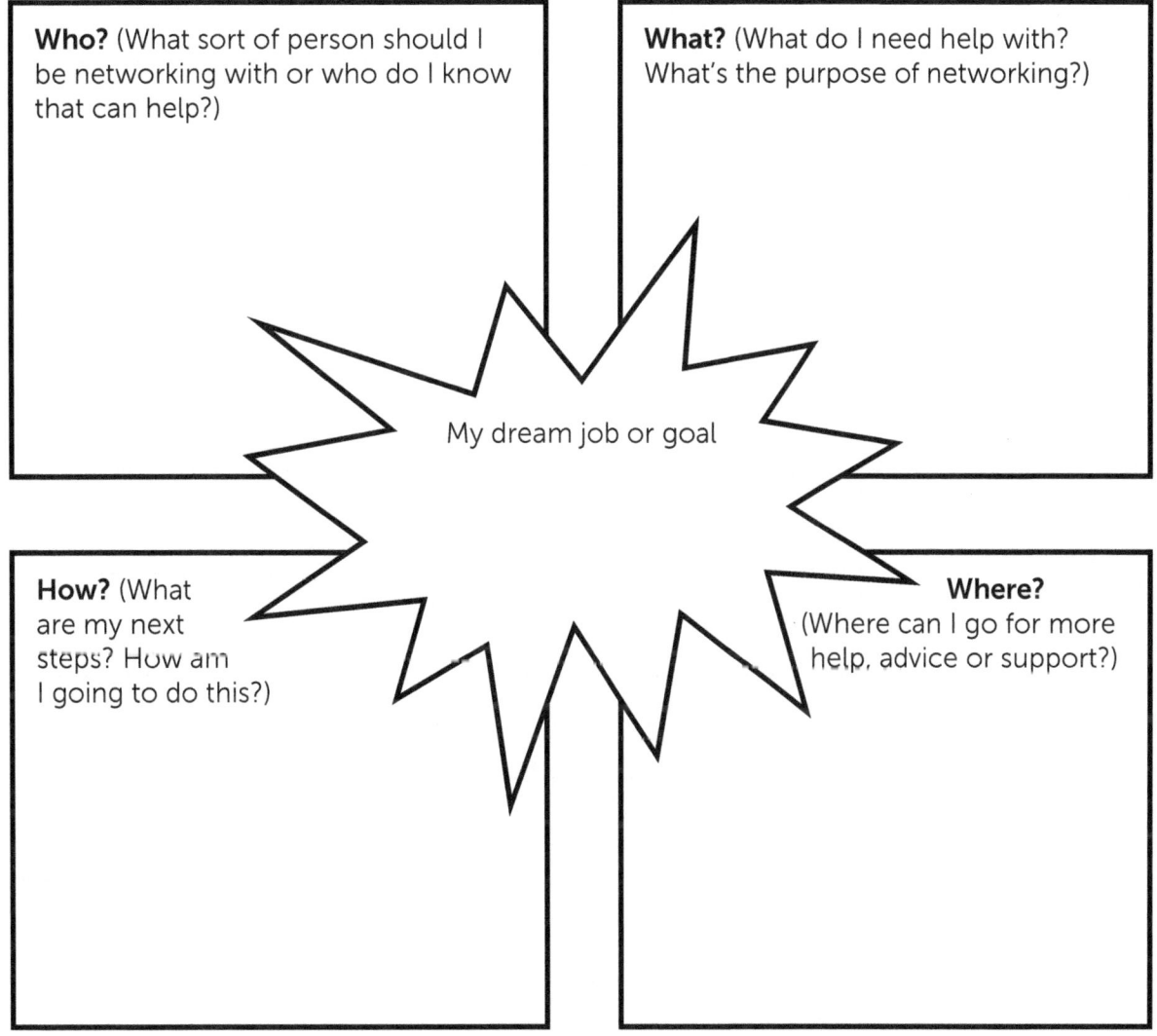

Resource 2.8
Find Someone

Practise networking with your classmates and find out what their dream job is, and the qualities, skills and experience they have that might help them reach this goal. Remember, networking is all about asking questions, being interested in what others have to say and listening!

Name	Personal qualities, skills & experience	Their dream job

Resource 2.9
Agree–Disagree Labels

Agree

Disagree

Don't Know

Resource 2.10
First Impressions

What kind of first impression do you make? Read the words below and circle three to five words that you think best describe the first impression you make. Be as honest as you can! You can also add your own ideas.

Confident	Bored
Chatty	Humorous
Happy	Polite
Young	Charming
Unconfident	Fearful
At ease	Ambitious
Intelligent	Unambitious
Shy	Successful
Nervous	Lacking direction
Relaxed	Purposeful
Anxious	Bossy
Worried	Talkative
Optimistic	Quiet
Smart	Tongue-tied
Wealthy	Negative
Educated	Lazy
Polished	
Natural	

Theme 3

Dream Building

Young people are rarely provided the opportunity to think positively about the future, and to cultivate openness to new opportunities, beyond education. For many youth, the future is an unknown prospect that needs to be figured out quickly. Theme 3: Dream Building helps young people to connect with their passions and purpose, exploring their inner drive and desires to create a vision for the future that is exciting, open to change, and diverse.

Learning objectives

By the end of this module, students will:

- acknowledge that their future is within their control, identifying their unique path to self-fulfilment
- expand their awareness about the possibilities for the future
- identify their own vision for the future, based on their goals, dreams, interests and values
- gain a clearer view of the range of opportunities available to them.

Activities

- Vision Boards
- Visioning the Future
- Wants versus Needs
- Creative Visualisation
- Five Years from Now
- Dream Inspiration.

THEME 3: DREAM BUILDING

Activity 1: Vision Boards
DREAM BUILDING

> **Learning objectives** *To explore the concept of creating a positive vision for the future*
> *To identify and explore our personal dreams and desires for the future*
> *To explore creative methods to set goals and think about our future*
>
> **Resources required** *A selection of magazines/newspapers; coloured paper; marker pens; scissors; glue; poster board or card*

SET THE SCENE

Introduce the theme for this section of activities – dream building.

Ask students what it means to have a dream. Why is it important to dream?

This activity will help students to think broadly about what is important to them, identifying hopes and dreams for the future. Having dreams can help us to be forward-thinking, take positive action and keep going when we feel disheartened.

EXPLORE

Explain to students that they will create a vision board. Ask if anyone has seen or made a vision board before, and what they think it might be.

A vision board is a collage of images and words that represent a person's hopes and dreams. There is no right or wrong way to create one. Provide students with a selection of magazines, newspapers, coloured paper, marker pens, scissors and glue, and poster board or a large sheet of card to use as their board.

There are lots of examples of vision boards online which might inspire anyone who gets stuck.

Students can think about their long-term and short-term dreams, which may be related to their career, family, travel, appearance and other goals.

TAKE IT FORWARD

Ask students to share their vision boards, explaining what the images and words represent.

Discuss:

- Is it important to think about dreams and the future? Why?
- Was anyone surprised by something they added to their dream board?
- How do you feel, looking at your vision board?

Activity 2: Visioning the Future
DREAM BUILDING

Learning objectives	*To explore the concept of core values*
	To explore how our goals and visions for the future represent emotional needs and meeting our values
	To explore the intrinsic values of external success
	To encourage students to explore how to reflect their values in everyday life
Resources required	*Paper; marker pens; Resource 3.1: List of Values*

SET THE SCENE

Ask students to display their vision boards (created in the last activity) in front of them. In this activity they will go a little deeper to explore what dreams and goals their vision board really represents.

EXPLORE

Give each student a piece of paper and ask them to split it into three columns. In the first column they should list the main themes or dreams they have included in their vision board, e.g. owning a large home, becoming a doctor or travelling to India.

When they have created their list, ask the students to list the feeling they experience when thinking about each dream in the second column. What emotion do they experience when they take time to imagine that dream is a reality?

Next, ask students to write in the third column what important value the dream represents. You may wish to explore the concept of values with students. Our values are the things most important to us in life, e.g. independence, peace, love or success.

If needed, hand out copies of *Resource 3.1: List of Values*. Encourage students to unpick their values as much as possible to get to the core of what the dream represents for them. For example, a dream of owning a fast car might seem at first to represent a value of being wealthy, but upon further thought being wealthy actually represents a value of security.

Finally, looking at their three lists, ask students to circle which dreams are most important to them. Which dreams are in reach now and which are further away?

TAKE IT FORWARD

Discuss:

- What does your vision board represent?
- Which are your most important dreams?
- How would your life be different if those dreams were a reality?
- Are there other ways you can create the feelings and reflect the values your dream represents in your life now?
- What steps could you take towards making your dream a reality?

Activity 3: Wants versus Needs
DREAM BUILDING

> **Learning objectives** *To explore the concept of personal needs and wants*
> *To identify examples of wants and needs*
> *To explore the differences between wants and needs*
>
> **Resources required** *Large sheet of paper and/or whiteboard; marker pens;*
> *Resource 3.2: Wants versus Needs cut up into rectangles*

SET THE SCENE

Ask students to suggest the difference between a want and a need. Ask students to suggest some examples of wants and needs and record these on the whiteboard or on a large sheet of paper.

EXPLORE

Split the students into groups of four to six. Print one copy of *Resource 3.2* for each group, and cut up each word or phrase into a label. Students should work together to identify which are examples of wants (things we desire but can live without), and which are examples of human needs (things we need to live safe, happy, healthy lives), placing the labels into two columns.

When complete, ask each group to feed back their answers and discuss as a whole group to find consensus.

Ask students to refer back to their vision boards created in *Activity 1*. Looking at their dreams recorded on the board, discuss which represent wants and which represent needs.

TAKE IT FORWARD

Discuss:

- Do our wants fulfil a need?

- Is there a better way to get those needs met?

Activity 4: Creative Visualisation
DREAM BUILDING

> **Learning objectives**   *To explore the concept of creative visualisation as a tool for positive thinking and planning for the future*
> *To practise using creative visualisation to positively focus the mind on future goals and success*
>
> **Resources required**   *Resource 3.3: Creative Visualisation Script*

SET THE SCENE

Ask students if they have heard the term 'creative visualisation' before. Creative visualisation is the process of using your imagination and focusing on images in your mind, in a state of relaxation, to bring about what you desire in your life. Visualisation helps to put us in a positive frame of mind to reach our goals.

Sometimes our minds become too focused on negative thoughts or worries, or we get caught up in daily life and forget to think about our goals and dreams. Visualisation helps us to focus on what we want in life, and to put ourselves in a positive state to receive it.

EXPLORE

Create a safe, quiet place to conduct the visualisation. Encourage students to close their eyes and relax, but stress that they can open their eyes and stop at any time. This is not a hypnosis or state-changing exercise in any way, simply the process of focusing the mind on a positive thought. You can add detail and specific information into a visualisation to meet the needs of your specific students.

Read aloud the script in *Resource 3.3*, using a calm, soft tone of voice. Read the script slowly, pausing to allow the students to visualise as you read. Be ready to stop if a young person appears uncomfortable or agitated. The script asks the young person to visualise their positive future and dreams, based upon the vision board they created in *Activity 1: Vision Boards*.

When complete, allow time for the students to reflect upon the process for a few moments, before encouraging them to open their eyes and stretch, slowly coming back into the room.

Discuss their responses to the process and any particular reflections or realisations they had, and remind students that they can repeat this process at any time.

ACTIVITY 4: CREATIVE VISUALISATION

TAKE IT FORWARD

Ask students to share their experience and reflections of the visualisation process. Discuss:

- How did you feel during the visualisation?

- Was it a useful process?

- Would anyone use this process again?

- How can visualisation help us to reach our goals and dreams?

THEME 3: DREAM BUILDING

Activity 5: Five Years from Now
DREAM BUILDING

> **Learning objectives** *To encourage students to consider their future goals and aspirations*
> *To explore our mindset about the future*
> *To identify the steps we need to take to move towards future goals and dreams*
>
> **Resources required** *Resource 3.4: Five Years from Now*

SET THE SCENE

Discuss:

- Who thinks about the future, and if so, how often?
- How does the future look in your mind? Is it largely positive or negative?
- For those who don't think about the future, why not?

Explain to students that this activity will help us to jump five years into the future to help us set and reach our goals.

EXPLORE

Distribute copies of *Resource 3.4: Five Years from Now*, one per person.

Students should start with the first part of the worksheet, thinking about life one year ago. Looking at each part of their life they should score it from 1 to 10 (with 1 being extremely dissatisfied and 10 being extremely satisfied) and write a sentence alongside to explain their score.

Next, they should complete the second part of the worksheet and repeat the same process but imagining their life five years from now.

TAKE IT FORWARD

Ask students to share their reflections from completing the worksheet.
Discuss:

- How do you feel looking at the scores of your past and the future life?
- Which is more positive? Why?
- What needs to change in your life to either increase your scores, or help to get you to those scores in five years' time?

Activity 6: Dream Inspiration
DREAM BUILDING

Learning objectives	*To inspire students to create a positive outlook for the future*
	To encourage students to identify their own sources of inspiration
	To encourage students to surround themselves with positive reminders to stay on track towards future goals
	To creatively express positive thoughts
Resources required	*Poster board or card; creative materials, e.g. marker pens, paints, magazines, coloured card, etc.*

SET THE SCENE

Discuss:

- What helps us to feel inspired?
- Who looks at positive quotes on the Internet, or shares positive quotes on social media? Why/why not?
- How do positive quotes help people?

Explain to students that this activity will help to remind us of our dreams by creating our own positive quotes or inspirational sayings.

EXPLORE

Give each student a piece of card and some creative materials, e.g. marker pens, paints, magazines, coloured card, etc.

Ask students to research or brainstorm their favourite positive quotes – access to the Internet may be needed for this – or encourage students to think of their own.

Ask each student to choose a favourite quote and write or draw it, decorating the card. The quotes can then be displayed in the classroom, or taken home.

TAKE IT FORWARD

Ask students to share their quotes and discuss what they liked about each other's work. Which words inspire us the most?

Resource 3.1
List of Values

Achievement	Pleasure	Security
Peace	Contribution	Job/Career
Competition	Truth	Freedom
Status	Nature	Personal
Loyalty	Community	Growth
Commitment	Integrity	Confidence
Honesty	Excellence	Trust
Education	Beauty	Money
Adventure	Health/Fitness	Communication
Fulfilment	Spirituality	Independence
Wisdom	Love	Empowerment
Intimacy	Recognition	Balance
Creativity	Leisure	Happiness
Solitude	Friendship	Respect

Resource 3.2
Wants versus Needs

Read the examples below and decide which are examples of 'wants' (things we *want* but can live without) and which are examples of 'needs' (things we *need* to exist and flourish as human beings).

The latest phone	Food
Friendship	Respect
Physical touch (e.g. hugs)	Clothing
Sleep	The latest branded (designer) sunglasses
Holidays and day trips out	Shelter (a home or a roof over your head)
Transportation (e.g. a car or bike)	Clean water
Money	Entertainment

Resource 3.3
Creative Visualisation Script

Create a safe, quiet place to conduct the visualisation, and ensure that you read the script slowly, with a soft and gentle tone of voice.

Close your eyes and breathe deeply, allowing your body to relax. Focus on relaxing each part of your body from your toes, to your legs, your knees, your stomach, all the way up to your chest, your arms, your neck and your head. As you take each breath in, imagine you are breathing in relaxation and positivity, and as you breathe out imagine you are letting go of any worries and stress.

Imagine you are living ten years in the future. The years have passed by in a flash and you are a whole decade older. Imagine looking in the mirror and seeing an older you reflected back. Your eyes are shining with excitement and energy, your face is smiling broadly with happiness, and you look relaxed and fulfilled.

Everything you dreamt about and wanted to happen has become a reality, and much more, beyond anything you could imagine. Look around yourself and see the home you are living in. You feel safe and secure, with beautiful objects and furniture around you and an amazing view from the windows, just as you imagined. Look closely and notice what you can see. Are there tall buildings and skyscrapers, or fields and trees? Can you feel the breeze blowing in from the bright blue ocean and feel the sun on your skin?

Notice what you are wearing. The clothes feel comfortable and fit you perfectly. You feel healthy and strong, your body is just as you wish it to be, and you can stand tall with confidence and grace, your head held high.

Step outside of your house and onto the street. You greet some friends – notice how happy you feel to have such a large circle of friends who care about you and want to spend time with you. You make plans to do something fun with them later. What is it?

You are going off to work for the day. How will you get there? Imagine yourself travelling to work, in a shiny new car, or walking, or perhaps by bus or train. Maybe you work from home. Imagine what you'll be doing when you get to work. Picture yourself with your colleagues and imagine how fulfilled you feel. You have a sense of purpose and you feel energised to be doing something good in the world and earning money.

Imagine yourself returning home at the end of the day. You feel tired but content, knowing you have worked hard. All those years of studying have paid off, and as you step inside your home you can see all of the things your money has helped you to buy. There are photographs on the shelf and on the walls from holidays and trips you have taken, and special occasions over the years. Who is in the photographs? Where are you?

Imagine who will be there to greet you when you get home. Do you live alone, or with friends perhaps, or maybe you have a family? Imagine them coming to meet you at the door with hugs and smiles. You fall asleep at the end of the day deeply satisfied and content.

When you're ready, come back into the room and slowly open your eyes.

Resource 3.4
Five Years from Now

Think back to one year ago. Consider the different parts of your life below and score each one from 1 to 10 (where 1 is extremely dissatisfied with your life, and 10 is extremely satisfied). Write a sentence alongside each to explain your score. Next, complete the second part of the worksheet and repeat the same process but imagining your life in five years' time. Be as honest and as realistic as possible.

One year ago	Score 1–10	Description
Physical health		
Mental health		
Friendships		
Home life		
School/College		
Love/Relationship		
Money		
Future plans		
Fun/Hobbies		
Appearance		

Five years future	Score 1–10	Description
Physical health		
Mental health		
Friendships		
Home life		
School/College		
Love/Relationship		
Money		
Future plans		
Fun/Hobbies		
Appearance		

Theme 4

Money Matters

Money Matters helps young people to understand money and personal finance, developing financial literacy and practical lifelong skills to manage money, create savings, explore budgeting and develop a cohesive understanding of the cost of living, thus influencing young people's perceptions about the type of job role or career they may seek to undertake. Money Matters aims to raise awareness of the basics and pitfalls of managing personal finance.

Learning objectives

By the end of this module, students will:

- understand the basics of personal budgeting and saving
- identify the dangers and pitfalls of managing money
- calculate their cost of living and income needed to maintain this lifestyle
- explore the language of finance, building young people's awareness of key terms
- explore ways to manage money as a young person, including opening a bank account, saving, and borrowing (e.g. student loans).

Activities

- Does Money Matter?
- Money Essentials
- True or False?
- Calculating Costs
- Savvy Savers
- Money Values
- The Cost of Living
- Budgeting Basics.

Activity 1: Does Money Matter?

MONEY MATTERS

> **Learning objectives** *To explore the value of money*
> *To identify the benefits and drawbacks to wealth*
> *To explore our values related to money*
> *To identify the limitations of money*
>
> **Resources required** *Large sheets of paper; marker pens*

SET THE SCENE

Introduce the theme of this series of activities: understanding money and finances. Explain to students that these series of activities and lessons will help them to be more savvy with their money, understand how to manage their finances and be aware of the dangers and pitfalls when dealing with money.

Discuss:

- What does money help us to do?
- What are some of the downsides or dangers to having our own money?
- Some people say 'money makes the world go around'. What do you think?

EXPLORE

Split students into groups of approximately four to six people and give each group a large sheet of paper and some marker pens. Ask the groups to split their paper into two and label one side 'things money provides' and the other side 'things money doesn't provide'. Ask students to think of ideas of things that money can buy or provide in life, e.g. a home, clothes, a new phone, etc. They should then consider what money *can't* buy, such as love, good friendships, health, etc. There may be some overlapping areas that are debateable, such as good health being an intrinsic, natural benefit that money can't buy, but could be improved upon by good healthcare which might need to be financed.

Come back together as a group and discuss the activity. Discuss:

- What did you notice about the activity?
- On a scale of 1 to 10, where 1 is not at all and 10 is very important, how important is money to you?
- Do we place too much importance on the things that money can buy? Why?
- Are there drawbacks or limitations to money? If so, what are they?

THEME 4: MONEY MATTERS

TAKE IT FORWARD
- -
Ask students to go back to their papers and circle their top three most important things they have written, on either side of the paper. Ask volunteers to share their top three. Explore whether those top three might change in time, or are likely to stay the same. How might those important things influence someone's life choices and future career path?

Activity 2: Money Essentials
MONEY MATTERS

Learning objectives	*To define and understand common financial terms*
	To explore our current and future use of money and financial services
Resources required	*Resource 4.1: Money Essentials Labels and Resource 4.2: Money Essentials Descriptions, cut into individual labels*

SET THE SCENE

Ask students to share (if they feel comfortable doing so) how much pocket money they receive each week. Does anyone have a part-time job or a way of earning money? Ask participants to share how they spend their money, if they wish to do so.

Ask students to raise their hand if:

- they have a bank account
- they have a savings account
- they have a debit or credit card
- they have a PayPal account or other online account to send or spend money.

Explore as a group how we learn about money and finances – who teaches us how to open a bank account or to take out a loan? This subject can often be confusing, and it can be dangerous to get it wrong. People can easily lose a lot of money or end up in debt through a lack of understanding.

EXPLORE

Split students into groups of approximately four to six people and give each group the terms found in *Resource 4.1: Money Essentials Labels* and then the corresponding labels on the first two pages of *Resource 4.2: Money Essentials Descriptions*.

Each group should work together to match the labels with the description for a range of common financial terms.

Come back together as a whole group and share the results.

The list of terms and descriptions on the third and fourth pages of *Resource 4.2* may be useful for some students to refer to throughout the activity, or can be used as a tool to develop understanding before the activity, if the facilitator provides copies for each student and explains each term to ensure students understand all of the descriptions.

THEME 4: MONEY MATTERS

TAKE IT FORWARD
- -

Ask students to reflect on whether they found the activity easy or difficult.
Discuss:

- Were any of the terms unfamiliar or new to you?

- What could be the dangers or downsides to being unfamiliar with these financial terms and services?

- Does being better informed mean we make better financial choices?

Activity 3: True or False?
MONEY MATTERS

> **Learning objectives** *To explore the facts and myths about money*
> *To develop confidence discussing financial terms and language*
> *To debunk unhelpful or inaccurate ideas about personal finance*
>
> **Resources required** *Resource 4.3: True or False Labels; sticky tack*

SET THE SCENE

This activity will help us to identify some of the truths and myths surrounding money, debt and finance. Often the misunderstandings or miscommunications about money can leave people confused, and can result in people 'burying their heads' about personal finance, which can lead to even greater problems.

Explain to students that they will play a game called True or False. It doesn't matter if they are unsure of the answer, the most important part of the game is to have a go and to learn something new.

EXPLORE

Place the 'True' and 'False' labels found in *Resource 4.3* at either end of the room. Explain to students that you will read aloud a list of statements and they have to decide whether the statement is true or false. They must 'vote with their feet', going to stand at either end of the room to correspond with whether they think the statement is true or false. After each statement, ask students for their feedback as to why they think it's true or false, and present the answer. Encourage discussion, particularly if the answer surprised the group.

Statements

1. Two-thirds of adults in the UK (66%) feel too confused to make the right choices about their money. (TRUE: LearnDirect study, 2011)

2. If you take out a student loan from the government, one day it'll just be written off (wiped away) if you don't pay it back. (FALSE)

3. You have to be over the age of 16 to open up a bank account in the UK. (FALSE)

4. You have to be over the age of 16 to take out a credit card in the UK. (FALSE)

5. 276 people each day are declared insolvent or bankrupt, i.e. they don't have enough money to pay their debts and bills. (TRUE: this is equivalent to one person every 6 minutes and 13 seconds; The Money Charity, 2018b)

6. It costs on average £20 per day to raise a child from birth to the age of 21. (FALSE: it is actually £30.23 per day; The Money Charity, 2018a)

7. It will take 26 years to pay off an average credit card debt in the UK with minimum repayments, i.e. just paying off the minimum amount the credit card company will accept. (TRUE: The Money Charity, 2018a)

8. Your bank is legally required to refund all your money if you're the victim of a scam. (FALSE: The Money Advice Service, 2018)

9. If a bank goes bust you'll lose all of the money in your account. (FALSE: in the UK under the Financial Services Compensation Scheme (FSCS), if a bank fails you are guaranteed to get back up to £85,000 per person, per financial institution; Moneysaving Expert, 2017).

TAKE IT FORWARD

Ask students to share their thoughts about the activity.
Discuss:

- What surprised you?

- What did you already know? What didn't you know?

- What might help people who are in debt or worrying about money?

- How can we make good choices about our personal finances and money?

Activity 4: Calculating Costs
MONEY MATTERS

> **Learning objectives**   *To explore the concept of borrowing and lending*
> *To define and understand key terminology related to borrowing and lending*
> *To calculate the cost of borrowing*
> *To identify the pitfalls and dangers of borrowing money*
>
> **Resources required**   *Resource 4.4: Borrowing and Lending Cheat Sheet;*
> *Resource 4.5: Calculating Costs Case Studies*

SET THE SCENE

Explain to students that they will now begin to look at the cost of borrowing money, and understand key financial terms related to borrowing and lending.

Discuss:

- Who can you borrow money from if you need some extra cash?
- Why do people borrow money from banks and other institutions?
- Why do banks lend the money?

Encourage young people to understand that banks and other institutions don't lend money to people from the goodness of their hearts! They are making money on each transaction, in the form of interest payments, arrangement fees and other methods.

Encourage young people to identify the range of ways people borrow money — not just borrowing cash from friends and family, but taking out credit cards, mortgages to buy a home, car loans, general loans for different purposes, etc. Make a list of the different ways people borrow money and display it somewhere prominent for everyone to see.

EXPLORE

Split students into groups of approximately four to six people and give each group the 'cheat sheet' found in *Resource 4.4*, explaining key borrowing and lending terms, and the case studies found in *Resource 4.5*.

Each group should work together to calculate the cost of borrowing for each person described in the case studies.

TAKE IT FORWARD

Ask students to share their findings. Which people should borrow the money? Which shouldn't borrow the money?

Discuss:

- What are the benefits of borrowing?

- What are the downsides?

- What would help you to make an informed decision about borrowing?

Activity 5: Savvy Savers
MONEY MATTERS

> **Learning objectives** *To explore the concept of saving*
> *To define and understand key terminology related to saving*
> *To explore the benefits of saving money and ways in which to save*
>
> **Resources required** *Resource 4.6: Saving Case Studies*

SET THE SCENE

Introduce the theme of this activity: saving. Ask participants to share (if they feel comfortable in doing so) whether they are a saver. Does anyone save money, and if so, how do they save?

Encourage students to share the different ways of saving money, e.g. saving cash at home, putting money in a bank account, putting money in a savings account, investing, or saving online, e.g. in a PayPal account or similar.

Discuss:

- Why do people save?
- What are the safest ways to save money?
- Why do banks provide people with free savings accounts?

Help students to acknowledge that, as with lending money, banks want us to save our money with them so they ultimately have more cash at their disposal. It is to the bank's benefit to have our money in their account.

EXPLORE

Split students into groups of approximately four to six people, give each group a copy of *Resource 4.6: Saving Case Studies* and ask them to calculate how much each person is saving in the case studies presented. Students may wish to refer to the cheat sheet in *Resource 4.4* which explains key terms.

TAKE IT FORWARD

Ask students to share their findings. Is it always a good idea to save? Explore how saving might make us feel, and how spending can make us feel. Each can provide the same positive emotions, although spending can give a more immediate hit of happiness or thrill. Ultimately this needs to be balanced up with the long-term pain if too much spending leads to debt and other problems.

THEME 4: MONEY MATTERS

Activity 6: Money Values
MONEY MATTERS

> **Learning objectives**   *To explore the concept of values in relation to money and finances*
> *To define and explore our personal values*
> *To debate our values to gain perspectives from others*
>
> **Resources required**   *Resource 2.9: Agree–Disagree Labels; sticky tack*

SET THE SCENE

Money can be a complex topic. Although it's been around for thousands of years in different forms, money can still cause wars and conflict, break up relationships, cause heartache and misery, as well as offer great experiences and luxuries, enable us to help others and do good in the world, enrich our lives and make them easier, and so much more.

Explain to students that this activity will encourage us to debate and explore our values about money.

EXPLORE

Place the 'Agree' and 'Disagree' labels found in Resource 2.9 (previously used in a Theme 2 activity) at either end of the room, with the 'Don't Know' label in the middle of the room. Explain to students that you will read aloud some scenarios that will encourage us to think about our values about money.

There are no right or wrong answers, just our opinions. Encourage debate by asking students to share why they chose to agree, disagree, or don't know.

Scenarios

- If you found a wallet on the street you should hand it in to the police.
- It's OK to keep cash if you found it on the street.
- It's better to take a job you love with lower pay over a job with better pay but that you would not be as happy in.
- You should never lend money to friends or family.
- Money is a private matter and shouldn't be discussed with friends, family or a partner.
- It's better to splurge and buy what you want in life, as you can't take it with you when you're gone.

- If you borrow money from a bank or take out a credit card and then can't afford to pay it back, it doesn't really hurt anyone – these big companies have lots of money.

- Borrowing more money when you're already in debt is a vicious cycle that will lead to bigger and bigger problems.

TAKE IT FORWARD

Ask students to share their thoughts about the activity. Do we have different views and values about money? Where do these values come from?

THEME 4: MONEY MATTERS

Activity 7: The Cost of Living
MONEY MATTERS

> **Learning objectives** *To explore the general cost of living*
> *To explore the salaries of various job roles*
> *To identify the income needed to maintain a certain level of personal lifestyle*
> *To encourage students to explore in real terms how their choices about education and employment can affect their future experience*
>
> **Resources required** *One copy per group of Resource 4.7: Job Labels and Resource 4.8: Salary Labels, cut into individual labels; Resource 4.9: Job and Salary Answers; Resource 4.10: Cost of Living Worksheet*

SET THE SCENE

Introduce the theme of this activity: exploring our income and expenditure to estimate the cost of living and how much we'd need to earn to maintain a certain lifestyle.

Ask students to share what they would imagine their future to look like in terms of:

- the type of home they'd like
- the car they'd like to drive
- how many holidays per year they'd like to take
- other things they'd like to do, have or buy.

Explain that we will look at the cost of all of those things, and balance it against the average salaries of different types of jobs in the following activity.

EXPLORE

Split students into groups of approximately four to six people and give each group a packet of the labels in *Resource 4.7* with different types of jobs listed. Each group should match up the job to the average salary labels in *Resource 4.8*. Each type of job corresponds with a general UK average salary per year. The answers can be found in *Resource 4.9*.

Some students may need an explanation of the different job roles listed, e.g. an engineer, to be able to predict their salary.

Come back together as a full group and reveal the answers. Ask students if they found the activity difficult or hard. Was anyone surprised by the activity?

ACTIVITY 7: THE COST OF LIVING

Next, distribute copies of *Resource 4.10: Cost of Living Worksheet*, either one per group or per person. Students should calculate their predicted average cost of living based on their average calculations for rent/mortgage, bills, car repayments, holidays, food, enjoyment activities, etc. Students can either calculate these amounts based on their best estimations or based on their current activities (how much they or their parents spend per month), or can use the Internet to research a more general national figure.

When they have completed a monthly budget, ask students to calculate the annual figure on the worksheet, and then calculate the salary they'd need to earn to maintain that lifestyle.

TAKE IT FORWARD

Ask students to share their thoughts about the activity. Was anyone surprised by the amount they needed to earn to maintain the lifestyle they want? Has this changed anyone's ideas about the sort of job they'd like to do in the future?

THEME 4: MONEY MATTERS

Activity 8: Budgeting Basics
MONEY MATTERS

> **Learning objectives**   *To explore the concept of financial budgeting*
> *To explore why people create a personal budget*
> *To identify ways to maintain a budget, and how money can be wasted*
> *To create a sample personal budget*
>
> **Resources required**   *Resource 4.11: Budgeting Basics Case Study; Resource 4.12: Budget Example*

SET THE SCENE

Introduce the theme of this activity: budgeting. Ask students to define the term 'budget'. What does it mean to budget for something or to have a budget? Why do people have household budgets?

EXPLORE

Ask students to work individually or in small groups to explore the case study in *Resource 4.11*. Students should read the description of how Sally spends her money, how she saves, and how she might be wasting money.

At the end of the case study students should decide:

- How is Sally wasting money?
- How much should she save each month?
- What should be her new budget for her outgoings?

Ask students to complete the final part of the activity by filling in *Resource 4.12: Budget Example*, to create a new budget for Sally.

TAKE IT FORWARD

Share each person's or group's ideas about how the case study example is wasting money and how they could alter their spending and saving habits to create a better budget.

Resource 4.1
Money Essentials Labels

Credit	Loan
Balance	Debt
Interest	Mortgage
APR	Budget
Asset	Expenses
Credit rating	Income tax
Credit card	Overdraft
Savings	Cheque

Resource 4.2
Money Essentials Descriptions

Money that a bank or business will allow a person to use and then pay back in the future, and an amount of money that is added to an account.
The amount of money in a bank account, at any given moment. It can also be the total amount of money owed to an organisation, such as a credit card company, loan company, mortgage lender, etc.
The cost of borrowing money. This is the charge for the privilege of borrowing money from a bank or credit card company, for example, typically expressed as annual percentage rate (APR).
The annual rate charged for borrowing money, or earned through investing money. It is expressed as a percentage that represents the actual cost of borrowing the money per year, e.g. 12 per cent.
A resource with economic value that an individual, company or country owns or controls. It can relate to physical items such as stock, computers, or an office, or cash itself.
An assessment of the suitability and worthiness of a person or organisation that wants to borrow money.
A method of payment using a small plastic card, which is linked to an account. It is issued by a financial company to a person to enable them to borrow funds to pay for goods and services without needing to have the money themselves up front, on the condition that they will pay back the original amount plus additional charges, unless the person pays in full straight away, in which case no additional charges are made.

The amount of money a person or organisation has in the bank that is typically kept separately from day-to-day spending. It is used for a special purchase or as a safety net if needed.
An amount of money that is given to a person or organisation, for a fee, that must be paid back.
An amount a person or organisation owes to another person or organisation. This can also describe owing more money than a person has to give back.
A loan which is typically used to buy a house or land. The person borrows money from the bank to receive a large amount of cash up front to pay for the house, which they will then pay back over a long time span (typically 25–30 years).
An estimate of income and expenditure for a set period of time, e.g. a month or year. This is usually in the form of a spreadsheet or document to plan how much money will be coming in and going out, so a person or organisation can be sensible with their spending and saving.
The amount of money being spent or going out of a person's bank account.
A tax levied by a government directly on a person's income. A certain portion of a person's salary will go directly to the government to pay for things like healthcare, roads and infrastructure, street cleaning, schools and libraries, etc.
An agreed amount of money that a bank will lend to a person when their bank account balance reaches zero. This means a person can borrow a set amount of money when they need to, and no more.
A method of payment. A small paper-based document that orders a bank to pay a specific amount of money from a person's account to the person whose name is written on the document.

MONEY ESSENTIALS TERMS AND DESCRIPTIONS

- **Credit:** Money that a bank or business will allow a person to use and then pay back in the future, and an amount of money that is added to an account.

- **Balance:** The amount of money in a bank account, at any given moment. It can also be the total amount of money owed to an organisation, such as a credit card company, loan company, mortgage lender, etc.

- **Interest:** The cost of borrowing money. This is the charge for the privilege of borrowing money from a bank or credit card company, for example, typically expressed as annual percentage rate (APR).

- **APR:** The annual rate charged for borrowing money, or earned through investing money. It is expressed as a percentage that represents the actual cost of borrowing the money per year, e.g. 12 per cent.

- **Asset:** A resource with economic value that an individual, company or country owns or controls. It can relate to physical items such as stock, computers or an office, or cash itself.

- **Credit rating:** An assessment of the suitability and worthiness of a person or organisation that wants to borrow money.

- **Credit card**: A method of payment using a small plastic card, which is linked to an account. It is issued by a financial company to a person to enable them to borrow funds to pay for goods and services without needing to have the money themselves up front, on the condition that they will pay back the original amount plus additional charges, unless the person pays in full straight away, in which case no additional charges are made.

- **Savings:** The amount of money a person or organisation has in the bank that is typically kept separately from day-to-day spending. It is used for a special purchase or as a safety net if needed.

- **Loan:** An amount of money that is given to a person or organisation, for a fee, that must be paid back.

- **Debt:** An amount a person or organisation owes to another person or organisation. This can also describe owing more money than a person has to give back.

- **Mortgage:** A loan which is typically used to buy a house or land. The person borrows money from the bank to receive a large amount of cash up front to pay for the house, which they will then pay back over a long time span (typically 25–30 years).

- **Budget:** An estimate of income and expenditure for a set period of time, e.g. a month or year. This is usually in the form of a spreadsheet or document to plan how much money will be coming in and going out, so a person or organisation can be sensible with their spending and saving.

- **Expenses:** The amount of money being spent or going out of a person's bank account.

- **Income tax:** A tax levied by a government directly on a person's income. A certain portion of a person's salary will go directly to the government to pay for things like healthcare, roads and infrastructure, street cleaning, schools and libraries, etc.

- **Overdraft:** An agreed amount of money that a bank will lend to a person when their bank account balance reaches zero. This means a person can borrow a set amount of money when they need to, and no more.

- **Cheque:** A method of payment. A small paper-based document that orders a bank to pay a specific amount of money from a person's account to the person whose name is written on the document.

Resource 4.3
True or False Labels

True

False

Resource 4.4
Borrowing and Lending Cheat Sheet

APR

The annual percentage rate of charge (APR) is the cost of borrowing money over a period of a year. The rate, e.g. 5 per cent, is applied each month to the balance of a loan or credit card. This is effectively the price you pay (plus any other fees the bank or financial company places on top) for being able to access money you don't have.

TYPICAL APR

This is the rate most people who borrow money will be offered. The law states that at least two-thirds of all borrowers must be offered this rate.

REPRESENTATIVE APR

This is the percentage that is often displayed on adverts for a loan or credit card. It is the rate that is given to at least 51 per cent of people who take up the loan or credit card. Not everyone pays the same amount, and it will depend on a person's credit rating (see below).

Sometimes the APR can be written in small print or be confusing to people. Some short-term loans are offered to people with a poor credit rating at a huge APR, e.g. someone taking out a short-term loan of £100 at an APR of 500 per cent. This means that they will end up paying back £500.

CREDIT HISTORY CHECK

A credit history is a record of a person's repayment of their debts. A credit report is a record of the borrower's credit history from a number of sources, including banks and credit card companies. All of this information comes together to give an overview of a person's credit rating, which is how a creditor will judge whether or not this person is safe to lend money to. So if, for example, a person wants to take out a new credit card the credit card company will do a credit history check to see whether the person has paid back other loans on time, if they have missed payments, or if they have a lot of debt already. This will enable them to make a decision about whether to lend the money or not.

INTEREST RATE

An interest rate is the amount charged by a bank or loan company to lend money. It is expressed as a percentage of the amount the person wants to borrow, or 'principal'. Interest rates are usually calculated on an annual basis. For example, if a person wishes to take out a loan (principal) of £5,000 at an interest rate of 4 per cent, this means the borrower will pay 4 per cent of £5,000 per year.

An interest rate is also paid by banks when a person saves money with them. A bank will pay an agreed rate of interest on any sum deposited in a savings account, e.g. 2 per cent. This means if a person has £5,000 in savings they will earn 2 per cent of £5,000 per year, or £100. This is an incentive to encourage people to save money and deposit their money with a bank.

LOANS

A bank or other financial organisation will lend money to people or companies, if they think they can trust the person or organisation to pay it back. This means they need to feel confident that you are good at paying your bills, financially stable and trustworthy. Usually the bank will do a credit history check to see whether you've had problems with paying back loans in the past.

SAVINGS

Savings are the amounts of money that people put aside for use in the future after all their expenses have been paid. Typically people choose to keep savings in a separate bank account and add to them on a regular basis, to enable them to buy something new, such as a car, or to have a safety net in case of difficult times, such as losing their job.

Resource 4.5
Calculating Costs Case Studies

Jenny is struggling to make ends meet. She has no money in her bank account and her electric bill is due. She sees an advertisement for a short-term loan on TV. She can borrow £100 instantly, with the money being placed in her account on the same day. This seems like a perfect solution! She doesn't notice the small print on the advert which says the APR is 750 per cent.

Jenny has 12 months to pay back the loan, and must make a payment each month.

- How much will she pay each month?
- How much will she have paid back altogether at the end of 12 months?

Mike would like to buy a new car as his keeps breaking down. He finds a car he likes and the garage tell him that they can give him a loan at 6 per cent. Mike's bank is offering a loan at 4 per cent.

The car costs £3,000. Mike has three years (36 months) to pay back the loan.

- How much will Mike pay each month if he takes the loan from the garage?
- How much will Mike pay each month if he takes the loan from the bank?
- How much will he have paid back altogether at the end of the loan if he takes the loan from the bank?

Margaret and Bill are going to buy a new house. They have been offered a mortgage by their bank at an interest rate of 2.5 per cent. They can take out the mortgage for a period of 30 years.

The house they want to buy costs £150,000.

- How much will their monthly payments be?

- How much will they have spent on the house at the end of the mortgage term?

Danielle has a party to go to next weekend, but nothing to wear! She's seen a gorgeous new dress in her favourite clothes store but she has no money in her bank account. The shop assistant tells her that she can open up a store card (credit card) and take the item right now without having to pay a thing. The credit card's APR is 38 per cent.

Danielle's new dress costs £50 and she puts the amount on the store card.

- How much does the dress actually cost Danielle, with the fees charged by the credit card company?

Resource 4.6
Saving Case Studies

Lisa has just won £5,000 on the lottery! She decides to put it in a savings account with her bank. The bank's interest rate on savings accounts is 2 per cent.

- How much money will Lisa have in one year's time?

Mr and Mrs Williams have sold their house for £450,000. They are going to live with their son and daughter-in-law for a while, so won't need to buy another house.

They want to invest the money in a high-interest savings account, but they won't be able to access or withdraw the money for two years. The savings account offers a rate of interest of 7 per cent.

- How much money will Mr and Mrs Williams have in two years' time?

Enid's elderly sister recently died and left Enid all her money in her will. Enid is also elderly, and isn't very mobile. She rarely goes out much any more.

Enid's son tries to convince Enid to put the £15,000 she has been given into a bank account, but Enid doesn't trust the banks. Instead, she places all of the money under her mattress in her bedroom.

- How much money will Enid have in a year?

Kelly has £3,000 of debt on credit cards. She is currently paying £150 per month in interest and fees and the debt isn't reducing much at all.

Kelly's parents give her £3,000 as a gift to help her out. Kelly can put it in a savings account which pays out 1.5 per cent interest.

Or, Kelly can use the money to pay off her debts on her credit cards.

- Which should Kelly do, save the money or use it to pay off her debts? Which will leave her better off in the long run?

Resource 4.7
Job Labels

Lawyer	Office manager
Software engineer	Civil engineer

Prime minister	Pharmacist
Train driver	High school teacher

Prison service officer	Nurse
Librarian	Hairdressing/beauty salon manager

Street cleaner	Beautician
Care worker	Cleaner
Nursery assistant	

Resource 4.8
Salary Labels

£55,000	£27,643
£40,400	£36,142

£76,762	£37,439
£47,101	£32,524

£26,496	£24,927
£26,252	£22,113

£17,402	£11,618
£12,650	£7,919
£11,734	

Resource 4.9
Job and Salary Answers

Lawyer – £55,000

Software engineer – £40,400

Office manager – £27,643

Civil engineer – £36,142

Prime minister – £76,762

Train driver – £47,101

Pharmacist – £37,439

High school teacher – £32,524

Prison service officer – £26,496

Librarian – £26,252

Nurse – £24,927

Hairdressing/beauty salon manager – £22,113

Street cleaner – £17,402

Care worker – £12,650

Nursery assistant – £11,734

Beautician – £11,618

Cleaner – £7,919

Resource 4.10
Cost of Living Worksheet

HOME

Description	Estimated monthly amount (£)
Mortgage/Rent	
Electric bill	
Water bill	
Gas bill	
Council tax/Local taxes	
WiFi bill	
TV Licence/Subscriptions	
Phone bill	

TRANSPORT

Description	Estimated monthly amount (£)
Car payment	
Fuel	
Repairs/Maintenance	
Bus fares	
Parking costs/Other	

INSURANCE

Description	Estimated monthly amount (£)
Car insurance	
Home insurance	
Other	

GENERAL

Description	Estimated monthly amount (£)
Groceries	
Appearance (hair, beauty, clothes, etc.)	
Household items (toiletries, cleaning, etc.)	
Enjoyment/Going out	
Gifts	
Gym membership/sports	
Savings	
One-off costs (furniture, holidays, etc.)	

TOTAL PER MONTH	£

How much would you spend annually, based on your monthly outgoings?

_____

How much would you need to earn each year to maintain this lifestyle?

_____

Resource 4.11
Budgeting Basics Case Study

Sally is 21 years old and in her final year of university. She lives with three friends in a house share – each person pays £450 a month in rent. Their rent used to be £350 each last year, and they know there are cheaper places to live, but Sally and her friends couldn't be bothered with the hassle of looking for a new house at the end of their second year of university, so it was easier to just stay put and pay the increased amount. They like the house and the area they live in.

Sally doesn't drive and her university campus is about a mile away. She's often late in the mornings, so she tends to get the bus, which costs £1.20 each way. When she gets off the bus, Sally usually picks up a takeaway coffee and croissant from a popular high street coffee shop for breakfast as she was too late to eat at home. The coffee and croissant cost £3.75.

For lunch Sally and her friends go to the café on campus and she usually has a sandwich, crisps and a bottle of water, which is a meal deal costing £3.

Sally has a mobile phone on a contract for £40 per month which she's had for three years. She often goes over the data she's allotted within her contract, and tends to spend an extra £10–15 per month as she doesn't always realise she's used up her data and each extra megabyte is very expensive. She hasn't bothered to check if a new phone plan would be cheaper.

Sally and her housemates pay to have the latest TV packages, including a sports package and a movie package. That costs each person £10 per month, on top of their regular bills of £20 per month.

Sally works part time in a clothing store in the city centre. It's her favourite shop and she has a 10 per cent discount. Sally often passes the time thinking about which new items she likes and creating a shopping list for herself. When she gets paid at the end of the month, she usually spends most of her wages of around £100 on new clothes from the shop.

At the weekend, Sally usually goes to the pub with her friends and spends between £10 and £20 per night on beer. She will then get a takeaway pizza or chips on the way home, costing between £3 and £10. On Saturdays and Sundays she will spend her time going shopping. Sally loves to read and will usually buy a new book every week, costing between £5 and £8.

Sally has an overdraft on her bank account and each month gets charged £25 by her bank for going over her limit by spending more than she has in the account.

Consider how Sally spends her money:

- How is Sally wasting money?

- How could she save money each month?

- What should be her new budget for her outgoings?

Resource 4.12
Budget Example

Sally is spending too much money each month, and is wasting money unnecessarily.

Write down what Sally is currently spending, and consider ways for her to budget to save money each month.

Description	Amount Sally is currently spending (£)	Ideas for how Sally could save money	Amount she could spend (£)	Savings
Rent				
Transport – bus fares				
Eating out – breakfast				
Eating out – lunch				
Eating out – dinner				
Shopping				
Going out				
Phone bill				
Household bills				
Bank charges				
TOTAL				

Theme 5

Influences

Theme 5: Influences helps young people to identify the range of positive and negative influences in their lives which may impact upon their future decisions and plans. From positive role models to negative peer influences, *Theme 5* activities help young people to become more discerning and aware, in order to make well-informed and positive self-fulfilling decisions about their future.

Learning objectives

By the end of this module, students will:

- identify the range of influences in their life which could impact upon their future, discerning which are positive and negative
- identify the skills and qualities of positive role models who can be an inspiration and guide for the future
- understand the concept of stereotypes and media influences on their perceptions of self
- identify and overcome limiting beliefs which may be a negative self-influence.

Activities

- Mixed Messages
- The Influence of the Media
- Stereotypes and Labels
- Positive Role Models
- Being a Role Model
- Limiting Beliefs.

THEME 5: INFLUENCES

Activity 1: Mixed Messages
INFLUENCES

> **Learning objectives** *To explore the concept of influences*
> *To define and explore positive and negative influences and how they might affect our thoughts, feelings and behaviours*
> *To identify the subtle and direct influences in our lives and the impact on our decision making and choices about the future*
>
> **Resources required** *Large sheets of paper and/or whiteboard; marker pens*

SET THE SCENE

It may not seem so, but our thoughts, feelings and decisions are often influenced by the world around us.

Discuss:

- Who, or what, might influence our thinking and decisions? (e.g. friends, family, role models, the media, celebrities, etc.)
- How might we be influenced by others?

EXPLORE

Ask students to list some of the main people in their lives who influence their thinking and decisions. Write this list on the whiteboard or on a large sheet of paper to refer back to.

Discuss the difference between subtle and very direct influences. How might someone be subtly influencing our thoughts and decisions? How might someone be more of a direct influence?

Ask students to suggest why we let ourselves be influenced by others. Is it always a conscious process that we are aware of? Sometimes we are influenced by the world around us without even realising it – such as being influenced by advertising, our community and our culture.

Split students into three groups and give each group a large sheet of paper with one of the following words written in the middle of each one:

- community
- family
- friends.

ACTIVITY 1: MIXED MESSAGES

Each group should spend some time discussing and exploring the messages they receive from each group of influencers – family, friends or their local community – regarding:

- school
- success/jobs
- the future
- money.

You may wish to spend some time discussing what is meant by the idea of a 'message' – i.e. an unspoken idea or a perception, or a more obvious and direct message, such as being told by a parent that 'people from around here don't go to university'.

Allow each group to brainstorm some ideas for five to ten minutes and then rotate the sheets of paper in a carousel format, so each group can consider each theme and add their own ideas. When complete, come back together as a whole group and share answers.

TAKE IT FORWARD

Discuss:

- Are these influences and messages largely positive, or negative, or a mixture?
- What are the consequences of these influences? What impact might it have on our lives if we choose to believe these messages?
- Do we influence other people's thinking and decisions? How?

Activity 2: The Influence of the Media
INFLUENCES

> **Learning objectives**   *To define and understand the role of the media in our decision making*
> *To explore common media messages and stereotypes*
> *To begin to discern how mass media can affect people's thinking and attitudes towards youth, success and the economy*
> *To encourage students to become more discerning consumers of the media*
>
> **Resources required**   *Selection of magazines and newspapers; large sheets of paper and/or whiteboard; scissors; glue*

SET THE SCENE

Discuss with students: what is the media? Make a list of the various types of media on the whiteboard or on a large sheet of paper.

Ask students to share if they use or interact with the following forms of media on a daily basis:

- TV
- radio
- magazines
- the Internet
- billboards
- newspapers
- social media.

Ask students to suggest why these forms are sometimes referred to as 'mass media'. Who controls what appears in the media?

EXPLORE

Split students into groups of five to seven and give each group a selection of current magazines and newspapers, and access to the Internet and a printer if possible.

Each group will also need a large sheet of paper, some scissors and glue. The purpose of the exercise is to explore how the media represents young people and their future, and to explore how the media might influence their thinking about jobs, education, success and the future.

Each group should create a collage on one of the following themes:

- how the media represents young people
- how the media represents our country's economy/jobs
- how the media represents education and success.

Each group should cut out any articles, pictures or headlines that represent their theme and stick them onto their large sheet of paper, until it is filled. They should consider any stereotypical images and messages they see or, if this is a difficult concept to understand initially, they should just focus on finding any references to their themes in the magazines, newspapers and in online news.

TAKE IT FORWARD

Ask each group to share their collage and discuss any common themes in the articles, headlines and images they found.

- How are young people portrayed in the media? Is this accurate and true to life?
- How are the economy and job market in this country represented in the media? Does it make you feel optimistic or concerned?
- How are education and success presented by the media? Does the media provide us with certain ideas about what success is or should be?
- Are any of these ideas stereotypical and inaccurate?
- What are the consequences or impact of constantly seeing and hearing these ideas in the media?

THEME 5: INFLUENCES

Activity 3: Stereotypes and Labels
INFLUENCES

> **Learning objectives** *To define and understand the term 'stereotype'*
> *To explore common stereotypes and judgements*
> *To identify the impact of stereotypes*
> *To consider the stereotypes and judgements placed upon us*
>
> **Resources required** *Resource 5.1: Stereotype Labels and Descriptions; Resource 5.2: Speech Bubbles (photocopied and cut out: enough for at least three to four speech bubbles per person); sticky tack*

SET THE SCENE

Ask students to share what the term 'stereotype' means. What is a stereotype?

A stereotype is a label placed upon a group of people that presents a fixed and oversimplified image or idea which may not necessarily be true. Stereotypes can be based on a person's gender, sexual orientation, religion or race; for example, 'all girls like pink' or 'all men like sports'.

Ask students to share some examples of common stereotypes and discuss whether these are true or not.

EXPLORE

Distribute the photocopied and cut up labels found in *Resource 5.1* among the group, making sure each matching pair of labels are distributed to different people. Each pair of labels includes a type of person (e.g. mother) and a description of a stereotype about that person.

Give students five to ten minutes to read their labels and find their corresponding matching label, either a type of person or a description of a person.

Come back together and read aloud the matching labels. Discuss how easy or difficult the activity was. Why was this?

Stereotypes are usually well known and easy to recognise, and are commonly found in everyday life. Although we may know them to be untrue, sometimes we can believe a stereotype without questioning it, or fail to realise that the ideas we have about certain people are not accurate and are actually stereotypes.

Ask students to suggest some ideas for stereotypes (or labels) that may exist about them or that other people place upon them, either as a young person generally, as someone who attends their school or lives in their community, or more personal stereotypes that

ACTIVITY 3: STEREOTYPES AND LABELS

may exist for them because of their family upbringing, their past or their siblings (if they wish to share).

Distribute the speech bubbles found in *Resource 5.2* and ask students to write down as many stereotypes as they can think of, one per bubble. Provide some sticky tack and ask the students to tack the speech bubbles to one wall when they are ready.

TAKE IT FORWARD

Ask students to share some of the speech bubbles on the wall, either their own ideas or someone else's.

Discuss:

- Are these stereotypes and labels mostly positive or negative?
- How does it make you feel to read these labels and stereotypes?
- How might these labels influence how we see ourselves and the choices we make?

Ask each student to choose or identify a stereotype or label placed upon them that is holding them back in life, particularly in relation to school, their future and success. Ask each person to share if they feel comfortable doing so.

Discuss:

- How is this label holding you back?
- Is this stereotype true? Does it have to be true?
- What steps could you take to change the labels other people place on you?

THEME 5: INFLUENCES

Activity 4: Positive Role Models
INFLUENCES

Learning objectives	*To explore and identify positive influences*
	To define and explore the positive qualities of role models
	To explore the impact role models can have in our lives
Resources required	*Large sheet of paper and/or whiteboard; Resource 5.3: Success Case Study; access to the Internet for research*

SET THE SCENE

The previous activities have focused on some of the negative and damaging influences in our lives that can affect how we think, feel and view ourselves, which in turn can affect the choices we make and the paths we choose.

This activity will help us to focus on more positive influences, in the form of role models and personal inspirations.

Ask students to define and describe what a role model is, and does. How does someone become a role model?

Ask students to suggest some examples of positive role models, either someone they know or a celebrity. Record these on the whiteboard or on a large sheet of paper and ask students to identify the qualities of each person that make them a good role model, e.g. they are determined, respectful, supportive, etc.

EXPLORE

Distribute copies of *Resource 5.3: Success Case Study*. Working individually, students should pick a person they consider to be a good role model and a successful person (using whatever definition of success means the most to them). This person can be someone they know in real life or a celebrity/famous figure, dead or alive.

Students should research as much as they can about their chosen role model, creating a profile of them using the worksheet as a guide, including why they think the person is successful, where the person started from, where they are now, words to describe them, what they did to become successful, and why they are a good role model. If you do not have access to computers and the Internet to research role models, you may wish to set this as a homework exercise.

TAKE IT FORWARD

Ask each student to stand before the rest of the group and present their role model. They can use pictures and videos as well as their written worksheet if they wish to do so.

Activity 5: Being a Role Model

INFLUENCES

Learning objectives *To explore the concept of being a role model to others*
To explore the personal qualities of a role model

Resources required *Long roll of paper; marker pens*

SET THE SCENE

Ask students to consider what influence they have over others, including their peers, siblings, younger children and family.

Discuss:

- In what ways are you a good role model to others?

- Are there any ways in which you might be a negative influence in someone's life?

- Why should we want to be a positive role model to others?

EXPLORE

Split the students into groups of four to six and give each group a long roll of paper, as long as the tallest person in the group. Ask each group to choose one person to lie on the paper and someone else to carefully draw around them using a marker pen, to create an outline of a person.

When each group has created their outline of a person, ask students to turn their person into a positive role model. They should label their person to describe how a positive role model:

- speaks

- thinks

- feels

- behaves

- interacts with others.

THEME 5: INFLUENCES

TAKE IT FORWARD

Ask each group to present their positive role model and discuss any similarities and differences between the groups' ideas. Ask students to share how much they have in common with their role model drawing.

Discuss:

- Being a role model means setting an example for yourself and others. Why is this important in life and in the future?

- What might you need to do or change in order to become a better role model?

Activity 6: Limiting Beliefs

INFLUENCES

Learning objectives	To re-examine the impact of our beliefs on our thoughts, feelings and behaviour
	To identify the beliefs we hold about ourselves
	To challenge the validity of our beliefs
Resources required	Resource 5.4: Beliefs About Us; sticky tack; sticky notes; marker pens

SET THE SCENE

Ask students to share what a belief is, recapping on previous activities in *Theme 1: Believing in Me*. Where do our beliefs come from? How do they shape and influence how we see ourselves and the world around us?

Our beliefs are ideas and thoughts that we hold to be true and important – some people believe in a certain faith or religion, while others choose not to, but we all hold certain beliefs about ourselves, other people and our lives, e.g. we believe we are ugly, or attractive; or we believe the world is a safe, welcoming place, or a dangerous place we must protect ourselves from. Often our beliefs are in our subconscious – we don't think about them with our rational brain, but they are there, underlying and influencing our thoughts and feelings on a day-to-day basis.

EXPLORE

Hand out some sticky notes and pens to the group and place the four labels found in *Resource 5.4* on the walls around the room:

- Label 1: People from around here…
- Label 2: People like me…
- Label 3: Girls are supposed to…when they grow up.
- Label 4: Boys are supposed to…when they grow up.

Explain to students that they should complete each sentence, writing it on a sticky note and sticking it on or near the label on the wall. They can write as many sentences for each label as they wish – there are no right or wrong answers. Students should think about their own personal beliefs about each theme, whether they are positive or negative.

THEME 5: INFLUENCES

TAKE IT FORWARD
- -
Gather together as a whole group and read some examples of the sticky notes attached to each label.

Discuss:

- How does it feel to read these labels?

- How did it feel to write your beliefs?

- How might these beliefs influence your choices and your life?

- Can we change our beliefs?

Resource 5.1
Stereotype Descriptions and Labels

DESCRIPTIONS

My favourite colour is pink, I like doing my make-up and hair, going shopping and gossiping with friends.
My favourite colour is blue, I like football, I never cry or talk about my feelings and I get into trouble at school.
I shout a lot and tell people off. I'm in charge. I know a lot and I expect people to do what I say.
I do all the cooking and cleaning at home, I look after the children. I work part time and worry about my appearance.
I go out to work every day, I don't come home until late, I am strict and the head of the household.
I am 'girly', I hang around with girls and don't have male friends, and I've got a great sense of humour.
I like eating pizza and pasta. I like drinking wine. I talk a lot and wear designer clothes.

I am moody, selfish and anti-social. I stay in my room all day. I'm constantly texting my friends.
I'm very loud and friendly. I eat cheeseburgers and fries. I love sports.
I wear lots of fake tan, fake eyelashes and high heels, and I'm ditzy.
I live on a council estate. I do drugs and steal from others. I've been to prison.
I go to a church, temple or mosque every week, I say prayers, there are certain things I do not eat or drink.
I am afraid to go out at night, I am frail and fall easily. My memory is poor and I forget things. I am weak and feeble.
I am afraid of nothing. I'm tall and well-built, I'm a man and I have lots of physical strength. I am mean and look intimidating.

STEREOTYPE LABELS

I am a girl.
I am a boy.
I am a teacher.
I am a mother.
I am a father.
I am gay.
I am Italian.

I am a teenager.
I am American.
I am from Essex.
I am poor.
I am religious.
I am elderly.
I am a police officer.

Resource 5.2
Speech Bubbles

Resource 5.3
Success Case Study

Think of a person you consider to be successful (this might be someone you know, or a celebrity, sports person, etc.). Complete the worksheet about this person. You may need to ask them questions, or research the person online.

A person I consider to be successful is... _____

Draw a picture or print one to stick here

I think they are successful because...

This person inspires me because...

What did they do to become successful? Where are they now? What makes them a good role model?

Some words to describe this person are...

Resource 5.4
Beliefs About Us

People from around here...

People like me…

Girls are supposed to… when they grow up

★

Boys are supposed to... when they grow up

Theme 6

Career Curves

In the twenty-first century the concept of a job for life has all but disappeared, and many young people will find themselves navigating a winding career path across different roles, industries and even locations, as the nature of work continues to change and develop. Career Curves helps young people to understand the changing economy and world of work, and to become better equipped for a modern career.

Learning objectives

By the end of this module, students will:

- understand the ways in which jobs and the economy have changed and will continue to change

- challenge career and gender stereotypes, identifying outdated concepts that may still hold people back from achieving their future goals

- identify the skills and mindset they may need for a varied and diverse career path, which might be different to that of parents and grandparents

- explore the pros and cons of different types of modern work, developing awareness about the range of options available to them.

Activities

- The World of Work
- A Job for Life
- A Day in the Life Of…
- Career Stereotypes
- Gender Stereotypes

- Types of Work
- Career Pros and Cons
- Skills for the Job
- The Path to Success.

THEME 6: CAREER CURVES

Activity 1: The World of Work
CAREER CURVES

Learning objectives	To explore students' understanding of the world of work
	To explore how the job market has changed in the last 50 years
	To debate our personal opinions and perceptions about work and careers
Resources required	Resource 2.9: Agree–Disagree Labels; large sheets of paper and/or whiteboard; sticky tack

SET THE SCENE

Introduce this theme of 'Career Curves' by asking students to share what they know about the world of work. What does it mean to be employed? Ask students to share details about the jobs their family members do, or friends of the family. What do these jobs entail?

Ask students to share (if they know) what jobs their grandparents used to do, or what jobs were most prevalent 50 years ago. Make a list of these jobs on the whiteboard or on a large sheet of paper. Ask students to share what skills or qualifications they think were needed to do these jobs.

Next, make a list of the most common and popular jobs people choose to do today. What skills and qualifications are needed for these jobs?

Discuss:

- How has the world of work changed in the last 50 years?
- How might the world of work change in the next 10 or 20 years?
- What industries and jobs are no longer commonly found in this country?
- Which new jobs and industries have taken their place?

EXPLORE

Explain to the group that they will play a simple game to explore these ideas further. Tack the 'Agree' and 'Disagree' labels (found in *Resource 2.9*) on the walls on opposite ends of the room, with the 'Don't Know' label on a wall in the middle of the room. Read aloud the following statements and ask students to 'vote with their feet' and stand next to the label that matches their opinion. There are no right or wrong answers, but students should be able to justify and discuss their opinion.

Statements

1. To get a good job a university degree is more important than ever.

2. There are fewer jobs available for young people these days.

3. There is no such thing as a 'job for life' any more.

4. Doing one job for the rest of my life sounds boring.

5. Being your own boss (i.e. being self-employed or running your own business) is more secure than being an employee of a company.

6. Having any degree (even if it's not related to what you want to do eventually) is better than having no degree.

7. On-the-job training, such as an apprenticeship, is just as valuable as college or university qualifications.

Discuss students' responses and encourage debate and dialogue after each statement.

TAKE IT FORWARD

Discuss:

- Has the job market changed a lot in the last 50 years?

- How does it feel to be a young person who will be entering the job market soon?

- What are the most important actions a young person can take to become successful in the future?

- If you are continuing to the next activity in your next RfL session, for homework ask students to consider how the economy and job market in their country has changed over the last 100, 50 and 20 years.

THEME 6: CAREER CURVES

Activity 2: A Job For Life
CAREER CURVES

> **Learning objectives** *To explore how careers and the world of work have changed*
> *To understand the job roles, skills and qualifications needed in the past and future*
> *To encourage students to reflect on their perceptions of careers and work*
>
> **Resources required** *Resource 6.1: A Job for Life*

SET THE SCENE

Note: This activity will need introduction and preparation beforehand, as it involves tasking young people with a homework exercise to present in the RfL session.

Ask students to present their homework from the previous session, and discuss with students how the economy and job market in this country have changed over the last 100, 50 and 20 years. Ask students to share some ideas for how they think things have changed, and will continue to change.

EXPLORE

Provide each student with a copy of the worksheet found in *Resource 6.1: A Job for Life*. Students should use the worksheet as a guide to help them interview a grandparent or a retired person they know. The worksheet will prompt the student to ask questions about their career and employment history.

Ask students to bring their worksheets back to class so they can present their findings, sharing information about the person they interviewed and what they learned about their career history.

TAKE IT FORWARD

Discuss:

- Was anyone surprised by what they learned in this activity?

- Do the majority of the workplaces and industries employing our grandparents exist any more?

- What were the most valuable skills for the workplace when your grandparents were starting work? What would you say are the most valuable workplace skills now?

- How many people would consider following in the family footsteps and working in the same job or industry as their parents or grandparents?

Activity 3: A Day in the Life Of...
CAREER CURVES

Learning objectives	*To explore a selection of job roles and industries through the eyes of real employees*
	To explore how people progress in their careers
	To demonstrate positive social skills and presentation skills when engaging with adult role models
Resources required	*Invited role models*

SET THE SCENE

Note: This activity is extremely beneficial for students but will require planning on the part of the facilitator, as it requires inviting members of the public to meet with the students. Be aware of any insurance or background/police checks that may be involved with bringing adults into the classroom or to meet with young people, and never leave youth unattended with a member of the public.

This activity involves inviting representatives from various jobs or industries to meet with students, to provide a real-life and informal process for young people to learn about the real world of work. Although attending career fairs and events is extremely useful, bringing real role models and industry advocates into the classroom will help to facilitate more in-depth and informal discussions about the person's day-to-day work and the overall industry, allowing students to ask questions and learn more. Ideally you should invite three or four different adults to join the session, each representing a different industry; for example, a police officer, nurse, engineer and graphic designer.

EXPLORE

Before the session, explain to students who they will be meeting and what industries these people represent. Ask students to work in small groups to compile a list of questions they wish to ask, including questions about their:

- day-to-day role

- how they started in the job/industry

- their career progression (i.e. how they started, how they have progressed since, and where they may progress onto in the future)

- the skills and qualifications they need to do their job effectively

- any challenges they face in their job or industry.

THEME 6: CAREER CURVES

It is important to stress to students that they can still learn useful information from the visiting adults even if they don't represent a job or industry they find appealing or that matches their career goals.

Ask each visiting adult to share some information about themselves and their job for five minutes or so, and ask students to read their questions and make notes of the adults' answers.

TAKE IT FORWARD

Discuss:

- What did you learn during this session?
- Which role was most appealing to you? Why?
- Was anyone surprised by anything they learned about a job or industry?

Activity 4: Career Stereotypes
CAREER CURVES

> **Learning objectives** *To explore stereotypes about careers*
> *To identify our own stereotypes and limiting ideas about careers and jobs*
> *To explore the impact of stereotypes about careers*
>
> **Resources required** *Resource 6.2: Career Stereotypes; large sheet of paper and/or whiteboard; sticky notes; marker pens*

SET THE SCENE

Ask students to define the term 'stereotype'. This was explored in activities in *Theme 5: Influences*.

A stereotype is a label placed upon a group of people that presents a fixed and oversimplified image or idea which may not necessarily be true. Stereotypes can be based on a person's gender, sexual orientation, religion or race, for example, 'All girls like pink' or 'All men like sports'.

Ask students to suggest some examples of stereotypes that exist about jobs and careers, e.g. 'Hairdressing is a job for women' or 'Men are better bosses than women'.

Make a list of common stereotypes related to jobs on the whiteboard or on a large sheet of paper.

Discuss whether these stereotypes are accurate, and how it feels to read them.

EXPLORE

Tack the images found in *Resource 6.2: Career Stereotypes* around the room and hand out sticky notes and marker pens to students. Explain to the group that they should look at each of the images (representing different job roles) and write down their first thoughts that come to mind when they see each picture or consider the job being represented. These thoughts may be stereotypical or not, and may be positive or negative.

Students should write their thoughts on sticky notes and tack them on or around each image on the wall, writing as many thoughts for each image as they wish.

When everyone has finished, come back together as a whole group and discuss the thoughts shared.

THEME 6: CAREER CURVES

TAKE IT FORWARD

Discuss:

- How many of our thoughts about these job roles are stereotypical?
- Where do these stereotypes come from?
- Are these stereotypes true?
- How do these stereotypes influence our thinking about our future and our career decisions?
- What are the dangers of believing these stereotypes to be true; for example, that 'dangerous' jobs are just for men, or that women should stay at home while men go out to work?

TAKE IT FORWARD

Activity 5: Gender Stereotypes
CAREER CURVES

> **Learning objectives** *To explore and understand gender stereotypes*
> *To identify common gender stereotypes and explore the impact of such ideas*
> *To explore how gender stereotypes might affect people's choice of career or future choices*
>
> **Resources required** *Large sheets of paper; marker pens*

SET THE SCENE

Ask students what is meant by the term 'gender stereotype'. If a stereotype is a label placed upon a person or group of people, and gender refers to our biological sex, a gender stereotype is a generalised label placed upon women or men.

EXPLORE

Split students into two or more groups and give each group a large sheet of paper and some marker pens. Each group should brainstorm examples of gender stereotypes affecting males and females.

Ask half the groups to consider gender stereotypes affecting boys and men, and half to consider gender stereotypes affecting girls and women. You may wish to split the groups by gender, too. Students can consider general gender stereotypes, e.g. 'All women like to shop', and gender stereotypes relating to careers and money.

TAKE IT FORWARD

Come back together as a whole group and share ideas about gender stereotypes affecting each sex.

Discuss:

- Where do these gender stereotypes come from?
- How does it feel to hear these stereotypes as a girl? As a boy?
- How might these stereotypes differ in different cultures and communities?
- What can we do to overcome these stereotypes?

THEME 6: CAREER CURVES

Activity 6: Types of Work
CAREER CURVES

> **Learning objectives**   *To explore and define different types of employment*
> *To explore the pros and cons of different types of employment*
> *To explore why someone might choose to take a certain type of employment or voluntary position*
> *To build young people's awareness of the range of employment and volunteering options available to them*
>
> **Resources required**   *Resource 6.3: Types of Work Descriptions; Resource 6.4: Job Profiles; large sheet of paper and/or whiteboard*

SET THE SCENE

Ask students to suggest examples of the different types of employment or work people undertake, including paid and unpaid work. Display the following list on the whiteboard or on a large sheet of paper:

- full-time employment
- part-time employment
- fixed-term/contract employment
- volunteer
- intern
- self-employed
- freelancer
- apprentice.

Ask students to describe what they think each type of employment means. If needed, a list and full description of each type can be found in *Resource 6.3*.

Ask students if they know of anyone who is an intern, apprentice or freelance worker. What do they do for a living?

EXPLORE

Split students into groups of four to six and give each group a copy of the job profiles found in *Resource 6.4*. Students should read each profile and decide what type of employment each person might have, using the above list. Students should be able to justify their answers.

TAKE IT FORWARD

Come back together as a whole group and discuss students' thoughts about each profile. Read aloud the results from the job profiles and discuss how many they had correct or incorrect.

Discuss:

- Was anyone surprised by the many different types of ways to work or gain experience?

- Why might someone choose to volunteer or become an intern?

- Which is more secure, being a contract employee or being self-employed? Why?

- Which is more profitable, being a full-time employee or being self-employed? Why?

- What type of employment do you want to have? Why?

THEME 6: CAREER CURVES

Activity 7: Career Pros and Cons
CAREER CURVES

Learning objectives *To explore the pros and cons of different types of employment and work*
To develop more awareness about the different types of work in order to make informed decisions in the future

Resources required *Resource 6.5: Job Role Case Studies*

SET THE SCENE

Remind students of the various different types of employment explored in the last activity. You may wish to display the list and descriptions in *Resource 6.3* to remind students.

Explain to students that many people, particularly when starting out in their career after leaving school or college, think a full-time job is their only option. However, these days it can sometimes be difficult for young people to get a well-paid job in their chosen industry when they don't have much experience.

Ask students to consider some of the pros and cons of the different types of employment, and discuss as a group, e.g. the pros and cons of being a volunteer, an apprentice and a contract worker. What types of jobs or industries might typically employ people on a part-time basis? On a contract basis? As apprentices?

EXPLORE

Split students into groups of four to six.

Provide each group with one of the case studies found in *Resource 6.5*. Students should read the case study and list the pros and cons of the person's employment in the space below. For example, the benefits of being a volunteer – gaining experience to list on their CV; the disadvantages – lack of pay, and no benefits such as sick pay or holiday leave.

TAKE IT FORWARD

Ask each group to read their case study aloud and share their pros and cons. Ask if anyone can add any additional benefits or disadvantages.

Discuss:

- Consider your dream job. What type of employment might be best for you?

- It can sometimes be difficult for young people to get the skills, experience and qualifications they need for their dream job. What types of employment could a young person consider when starting out?

- Some people have multiple types of employment; for example, they work part time, they volunteer for an organisation, and they work on a freelance basis. Why might someone choose to do this? What are the pros and cons?

- Do you think the types of employment people choose today are different from those your parents and grandparents chose? Why?

- Are there more types of employment available today? Why?

THEME 6: CAREER CURVES

Activity 8: Skills for the Job
CAREER CURVES

Learning objectives	*To explore the range of skills needed in the workplace*
	To identify the specific skills and qualities needed for different types of roles
Resources required	*Multiple copies of Resource 6.6: Workplace Skills Labels cut up individually; Resource 6.7: Job Role Labels; sticky tack*

SET THE SCENE

Ask students to suggest ideas for the various skills, talents and strengths needed for the job market. What are the common skills and strengths needed? Which skills are specific to certain job roles?

For example:

- creativity
- determination
- organisation
- computer skills
- listening skills
- staying calm under pressure.

EXPLORE

Print out copies of the labels found in *Resource 6.6*. Each label describes a different skill, talent or strength needed in the workplace. You will need plenty of each label – ideally you should print them on sticky-back paper, or students can use sticky tack. Ensure students understand the definition of each skill.

Print the job labels found in *Resource 6.7* and tack them to the walls around the room. Briefly explore each job role to ensure each student understands what the job entails.

Provide students with a selection of skills labels and ask students to consider what skills each of the jobs would need. They should stick their label on or near the job roles. For example, a job as a police officer may need listening skills, the ability to be calm under pressure, and problem-solving skills.

Allow time for students to consider each job and come back together to review the skills and talents they think are needed for each role.

ACTIVITY 8: SKILLS FOR THE JOB

TAKE IT FORWARD

Discuss:

- Which of these skills, talents and strengths do you have?
- Consider your dream job: what skills and strengths might you need?
- How would you develop the skills and strengths you need for the workplace?

THEME 6: CAREER CURVES

Activity 9: The Path to Success
CAREER CURVES

> **Learning objectives** *To explore the actions needed to reach a career goal*
> *To encourage students to practise researching information related to their career goals*
> *To create an action plan to reach a career goal*
>
> **Resources required** *Resource 6.8: The Path to Success; access to the Internet*

SET THE SCENE

Note: for this activity you will ideally need access to the Internet for students to research the path to their ideal job.

Ask students to share their dream job, or a job or industry they would be interested in working in.

Discuss:

- What do you know about this job or industry?
- What are the entry qualifications needed to start within this industry or to get this job?
- How will you get from where you are now to this dream job?
- How can you find this information?

EXPLORE

Provide each student with a copy of the worksheet found in *Resource 6.8: The Path to Success*. Students should use the worksheet to help them explore the path to their dream job, or a job they are interested in researching. If students are struggling to identify a job or a career they are interested in, you may need to spend some time discussing their favourite school subjects, interests outside of school and their skills and talents. Activities from *Theme 3: Dream Building* should also help with this process.

Students should work individually to complete the worksheet, exploring their 'road map' to their dream job. They may need access to the Internet to research the qualifications and experience needed to do this job. You may need to demonstrate how to conduct an Internet search and provide examples of search terms.

ACTIVITY 9: THE PATH TO SUCCESS

TAKE IT FORWARD

Ask students to share their 'road map' and what they have learned.
Discuss:

- What are your first steps towards this career?

- What might be your next steps?

- Who could you talk to, to learn more and to create a plan of action?

- Where else could you find information to help you take steps towards this career?

Resource 6.1
A Job for Life

Find a grandparent or someone who has retired from work and ask them if they would be willing to be interviewed about their career. Ask the following questions or any others you can think of.

Person I am interviewing about their career: _____

What was your very first job?

How old were you?

What skills or qualifications did you need for the job?

How many jobs did you have in your working life?

What was the best job?

What was the worst?

For how many years did you do your last job?

Did you know what you wanted to be when you were young?

Did you have a choice about the career you would have or the job you would do?

What was different about the workplace when you started your first job?

What piece of advice would you give to a young person today?

Resource 6.2
Career Stereotypes

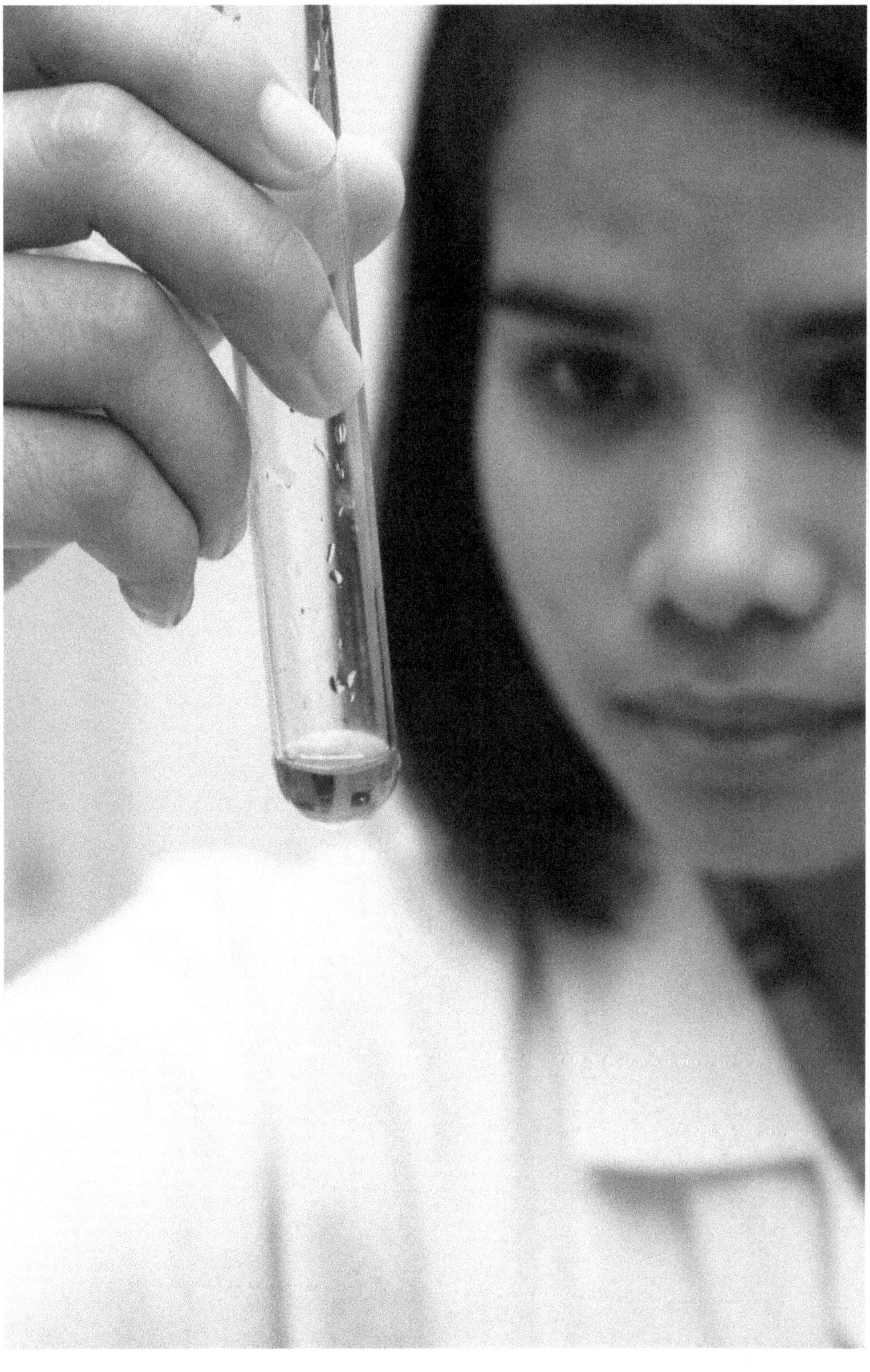

Resource 6.3
Types of Work Descriptions

FULL-TIME EMPLOYMENT

A person is an employee of a company, working on average between 35 and 40 hours per week. They sign a contract of employment, which means that they agree to certain terms and conditions (such as the type of work they will do, how many hours they work, how much sick pay and holiday pay they will receive, and so forth) and the employer also agrees to certain terms and conditions, such as paying them on the same day each month. Full-time employment often comes with benefits that are not typically offered to temporary or casual workers, such as paid holiday leave and paid sick leave.

PART-TIME EMPLOYMENT

A person is an employee of a company, working various hours per week, but less than a full-time member of staff. They will also sign a contract of employment, and will receive benefits such as sick pay and holiday pay. A part-time worker might be employed for 5 hours per week, or 25, depending on the position and what the company needs.

FIXED-TERM/CONTRACT EMPLOYMENT

Fixed-term or contract employment is the term used when a company hires an employee for a specific period of time. This might be to help with a project for six months or one year, or a shorter period, such as a few weeks. They will be contracted to help for that amount of time, and no more. The employer doesn't have to continue paying the person when the contract has come to an end. This can be beneficial for a company that can't afford to employ people for long periods of time (such as when a project ends or if the company is small). It can be beneficial to the worker if they like to be flexible with their time and do different jobs, but the downside is that the worker has less financial security and will need to look for work on a regular basis.

VOLUNTEER

A volunteer undertakes a specific job or helps out on a casual basis without pay. They may choose to do this because they feel passionate about a cause or what an organisation is doing, and/or they want to gain experience.

INTERN

An internship is a period of work experience that typically students or graduates do in professional roles, for little or no pay. The internship is usually temporary, for a short period of time (e.g. three months) and helps the intern to gain professional experience.

SELF-EMPLOYED

A self-employed person is a person who works for him/herself as an owner of a business or as a freelancer. They generate their own income by charging for services or selling products, instead of being paid a wage to work for a company. A self-employed person will be responsible for paying their own tax and keeping their own financial records, instead of a company doing so on their behalf.

FREELANCER

A freelancer is typically a self-employed person who offers their service to different organisations and companies for a fee. They are not employed by any company, and will get paid only for the work they do, for example offering graphic design services or web coding. They have flexibility and lots of variety in their work, but will not have any employment benefits, such as sick pay or health insurance, that people who are in full-time or part-time employment will have.

APPRENTICE

An apprentice learns a trade or skill from a qualified and experienced worker or organisation, typically in exchange for a low wage and for gaining knowledge and experience, for a fixed period of time. Apprentices are usually young and learning in a hands-on industry, such as mechanics or construction.

Resource 6.4
Job Profiles

Read the profiles of workers below and decide which type of employment they might be undertaking from the following list:

1. Full-time employment
2. Part-time employment
3. Fixed-term/contract employment
4. Volunteer
5. Intern
6. Freelancer
7. Self-employed
8. Apprentice.

1. Janice is 35 and has two young children. She works 18 hours a week at a local bank and has been doing the job for 12 years.

    Type of employment: _____

2. Sarah is an illustrator. She draws pictures for children's books and greetings cards. She works at home when she wants, and sells her designs to different companies and publishers.

    Type of employment: _____

3. Ben is 14 and is passionate about animal welfare. He helps out at a local charity shop on a Saturday afternoon for free.

    Type of employment: _____

4. Keri has just finished a three-year degree studying fashion design. She has been struggling to find work, but has been offered a full-time position with a top London designer for six months, as an assistant to a junior designer. She will not receive any pay.

    Type of employment: _____

5. Mike used to be a computer programmer for a big tech company but he left the position last year to start his own business. He set up 'Web Design 4 U' and designs and codes websites for different companies.

   Type of employment: _____

6. Jenny is a lawyer and works 40 hours per week for a law firm specialising in helping people to buy and sell property. She has 25 days of paid holiday each year plus sick leave.

   Type of employment: _____

7. Meena is 16 and wants a career in construction. She left school after completing her exams and instead of going to college she took a low-paid role with a construction company. She is 'learning while earning' and gaining experience from more qualified staff.

   Type of employment: _____

8. Jahal is a project manager, helping companies to organise, plan and deliver complex projects from start to finish. He is currently working with a big construction firm to help them coordinate a project to build a large block of flats. In two months he will start a new project with the government, who want to explore whether they can build a new road system.

   Type of employment: _____

Resource 6.5
Job Role Case Studies

CASE STUDY 1: JOHN (SELF-EMPLOYED FREELANCER)

John is a graphic designer. He was working for a marketing company, but times were hard and the company lost some of their big clients. They had to make John redundant (i.e. he was dismissed from the job as the company no longer needed him). John decided to become a freelancer and work for himself. He created a website to showcase his work and designed some leaflets and business cards. He sent them to everyone he knew and advertised on social media. John found some new clients who asked him to do some work. In March he earned £7,000 when a client asked him to do a big piece of work, but in April he only earned £50. In May he was asked to design a brochure for a big company, but he fell off his bike and broke his arm, which meant he couldn't work for six weeks and lost the work.

What are the pros (benefits) and cons (downsides) to John's type of employment?

Pros	Cons

CASE STUDY 2: SARA (INTERN)

Sara is 22 and finished university last year, gaining a degree in creative writing. She would love to write books but she needs to earn money to pay off her student debt. She sees an internship being offered with a publishing company in London for a publishing assistant role. It is a part-time role of 20 hours per week but is unpaid. Sara will gain lots of experience of publishing and will gain contacts to authors, agents and other publishers, and she has been promised a full-time graduate role when she completes the internship in six months.

What are the pros (benefits) and cons (downsides) to Sara's type of employment?

Pros	Cons

Resource 6.6
Workplace Skills Labels

Creativity	Computer skills
Determination	Listening skills
Organisation	Staying calm under pressure

Talkative and chatty	Artistic
Methodical	Fearless
Patient	Team player

Problem solver	Persuasive
Communication	Analytical
Confidence	Presentation skills

Honesty	Energetic
Gentleness	Maths skills
Respectful	Reading & writing

Resource 6.7
Job Role Labels

Primary school teacher

Carer for the elderly

Scientist

Neurosurgeon (brain surgeon)

Counsellor

Artist

Dental assistant

Outward bounds instructor

Civil engineer

Newspaper editor

Salesperson

Vet

Resource 6.8
The Path to Success

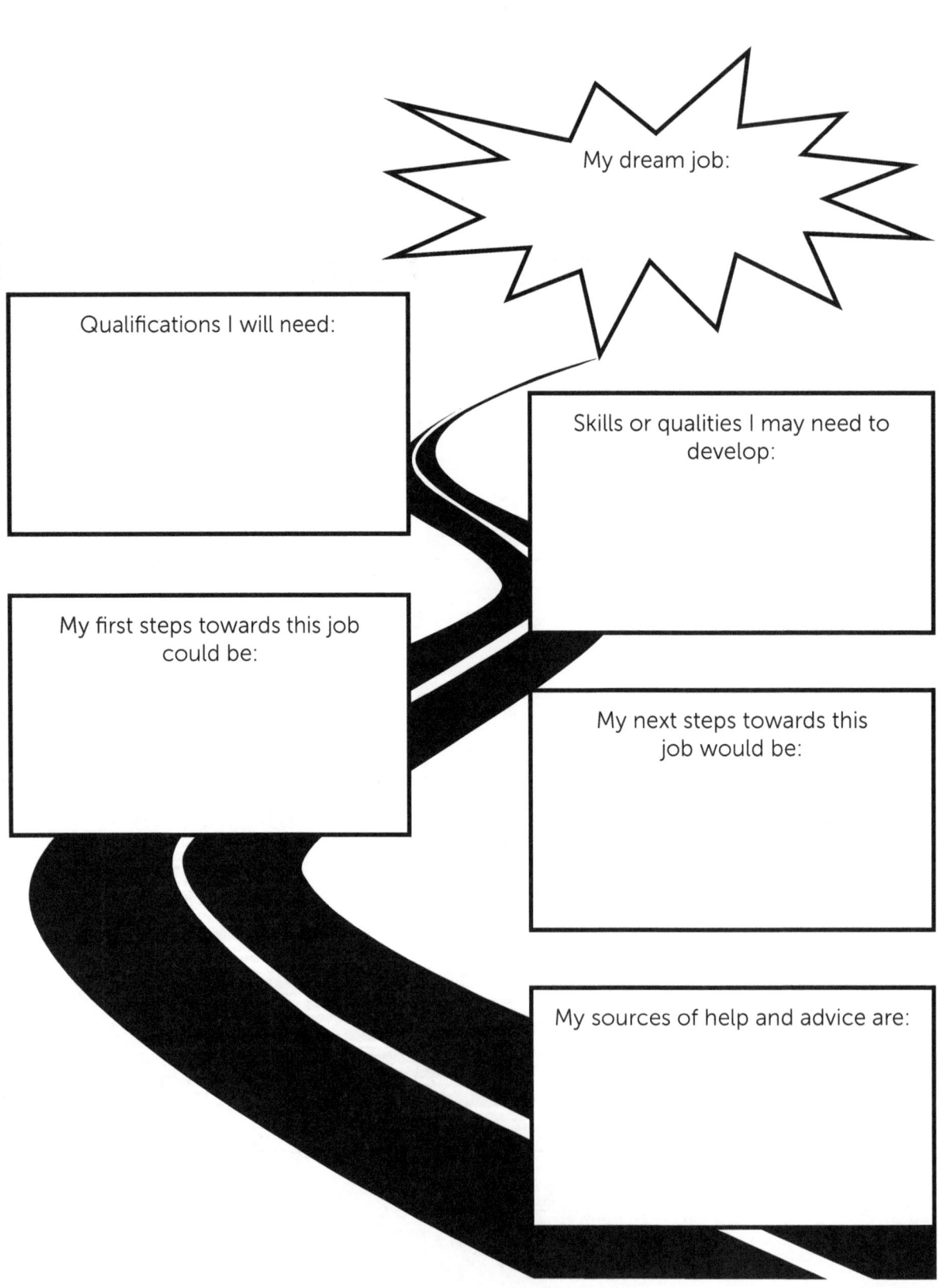

My dream job:

Qualifications I will need:

Skills or qualities I may need to develop:

My first steps towards this job could be:

My next steps towards this job would be:

My sources of help and advice are:

Theme 7

Business Basics

Entrepreneurship is a viable and successful career path for many people, and increasingly people around the world are turning away from traditional job roles to start enterprises that fulfil a passion, provide a work–life balance, or present more opportunities and income than a traditional job. Business Basics helps young people to explore entrepreneurship as a feasible career option, developing the skills and mindset of an entrepreneur.

Learning objectives

By the end of this module, students will:

- understand the concept of entrepreneurship and explore why people may choose to start a business

- explore the pros and cons to being an entrepreneur and identify positive role models who have circumvented traditional routes to build success in a different way

- develop basic enterprise skills, such as understanding profit and loss and conducting a SWOT (strengths, weaknesses, opportunities and threats) analysis

- explore ways to start a business now or in the future.

Activities

- Who Is an Entrepreneur?
- Budgets and Profits
- Big Business
- SWOT Analysis
- Profit and Loss
- The Branding Game.

Activity 1: Who Is an Entrepreneur?
BUSINESS BASICS

> **Learning objectives** *To define and explore entrepreneurship*
> *To consider and identify the key skills and attributes of successful entrepreneurs*
> *To explore entrepreneurship as another career path*
>
> **Resources required** *Resource 7.1: Entrepreneur Case Study; Resource 7.2: Entrepreneur Profile; access to the Internet*

SET THE SCENE

Ask students to share their ideas of what an entrepreneur is, or does. Can anyone think of a famous entrepreneur?

Ask students to suggest some ideas for how successful entrepreneurs got started. Was it luck? Skill? Determination? Or a combination of all of those things? Ask students to list some of the skills and attitudes needed to become a successful entrepreneur.

Ask students to share if they know anyone who is an entrepreneur – a family member or friend of the family, for example. Ask students to share some information about this person, including what sort of business they run and how they got started in business.

EXPLORE

In small groups, review the entrepreneur case study found in *Resource 7.1*. Students should review the case study and discuss the questions below. Come back together as a whole group and discuss the following points:

- Why do people become entrepreneurs?
- Having a good initial idea is important, but what keeps people in business and successful in the long term?
- What skills do entrepreneurs possess?
- What kind of attitude or mindset does an entrepreneur need?

Ask students to work in pairs and provide Internet access if possible, or set this task as a homework activity. Students should choose a famous entrepreneur and complete the worksheet in *Resource 7.2*, researching information about the entrepreneur.

ACTIVITY 1: WHO IS AN ENTREPRENEUR?

If students are struggling to think of an entrepreneur they might wish to research:

- Richard Branson
- Sir Alan Sugar
- Anita Roddick
- Simon Cowell
- Oprah Winfrey.

TAKE IT FORWARD

Ask students to share their entrepreneur research with the rest of the group.
Discuss:

- Could a young person like you become an entrepreneur right now? How?
- What did you learn about the entrepreneur you researched?
- Although there might be an element of luck to their success, what are the main qualities or attitudes you notice about these entrepreneurs that make them successful?

THEME 7: BUSINESS BASICS

Activity 2: Budgets and Profits
BUSINESS BASICS

> **Learning objectives** *To explore the basic tenet of running a business – creating a profit*
> *To practise setting a budget*
> *To explore how to make a product or service profitable*
>
> **Resources required** *Resource 7.3: Budget Planner; large sheet of paper and/or whiteboard; items to build a simple house, e.g. cardboard, paper, scissors, glue, sticky tape, etc.*

SET THE SCENE

Explain to students that the key to running a successful business is bringing in more money than you spend. You must have a profitable product or service that costs less to make or deliver than you charge for it to be able to remain in business, no matter how clever the product is, or how much the service is needed! This difference between cost to produce and the selling price is the profit. You may wish to write this on the whiteboard or on a large sheet of paper:

Selling price – Cost to produce = Profit (loss)

EXPLORE

Place students in teams of four to six people and explain that each team should work together to build a house. The house that is the best value for money and best designed (that can stand up on its own!) will win a prize. Each team should work together to plan their 'build' and can choose which supplies they will need to buy to build their house from the following list (you will need to provide these items). Students can also decorate the outside of their houses and be adventurous by creating a garden, garage or more!

Teams should use the budget planner in *Resource 7.3* to keep a track of their costs.

- Cardboard – £2.00
- Paper – £1.00
- Scissors – £0.50 per pair
- Glue – £1.00 per stick
- Sticky tape – £5.00 per roll
- Paperclips – £0.10 per paperclip

- Marker pens – £0.30 per pen
- Straws/sticks – £0.25 per straw/stick
- Coloured card – £0.50

When complete, each team should decide how much they are going to sell their house for, in order to make a profit. They will need to use the above equation to work out their profit. Students may wish to consider:

- the cost of materials
- how much other teams are charging – they will need to be competitive
- what they could do to increase their selling price, such as making their house more unique or special in some way
- how much profit they wish to make, without pricing themselves out of the market (i.e. making their house so expensive that no one will buy it because other houses are more reasonably priced).

TAKE IT FORWARD

Ask each group to present their house and their selling price. Compare budgets and discuss which house will have made the most profit if sold at the asking price.

Judge each house based upon the size, design and value for money, and introduce the winner. As a group, discuss if any of the houses are too highly priced, or are too cheap. What are our assumptions when a product is too cheap? (e.g. we may think the house has problems we can't see, or nasty neighbours!)

Discuss:

- Why is it important to keep track of your expenditure (outgoings) when running a business? (i.e. keeping a budget.)
- If you were building a real house what other types of expenditure might you have, apart from the costs of building supplies?

THEME 7: BUSINESS BASICS

Activity 3: Big Business
BUSINESS BASICS

> **Learning objectives** *To define and explore technical terms related to business planning and entrepreneurship*
> *To explore how businesses operate*
> *To explore what makes a business successful*
>
> **Resources required** *Resource 7.4: Business Jargon; Resource 7.5: Business Case Study*

SET THE SCENE

Explain to students that this activity will help them to learn more about business planning.

There are lots of different things to consider when starting a business, and writing a business plan helps entrepreneurs to carefully think through their idea and make sure it is financially viable and has the potential to be a success.

Provide students with a copy of *Resource 7.4: Business Jargon* and discuss as a group what each term means. They can use this resource to refer to during the activity.

EXPLORE

Working in pairs or groups of three, ask students to read the case study in *Resource 7.5* and to answer the questions below:

- What is the company's mission? (i.e. what do they intend to do? Why are they in business?)

- How will the business make money? (i.e. what are their main products or services?)

- Who are their main customers?

- How will they market their business? (i.e. how will they let their customers know what they have to offer?)

- Does this business have the potential to be successful, or not?

TAKE IT FORWARD

Ask each group to share their findings and discuss any common thoughts or themes. Discuss whether anyone would be interested in starting a business. How does running a business differ from being an employee of a company?

Activity 4: SWOT Analysis
BUSINESS BASICS

> **Learning objectives** *To define and understand the term 'SWOT analysis'*
> *To understand why a business conducts a SWOT analysis*
> *To define the strengths, weaknesses, opportunities and threats for sample businesses, and explore the real-life applications of such an analysis*
>
> **Resources required** *Large sheets of paper and/or whiteboard; additional large sheets of paper; marker pens*

SET THE SCENE

Explain to students that one of the tasks of deciding whether to start a business and writing a business plan is to conduct a SWOT analysis. Many businesses write a business plan and conduct a SWOT analysis to help them get funding, in the form of grants, investments or a bank loan. The SWOT analysis will help the funder to decide if the business is a big risk or worth investing in.

Ask if anyone knows what SWOT stands for, and write the following on the whiteboard or on a large sheet of paper: Strengths, Weaknesses, Opportunities and Threats.

A SWOT analysis helps entrepreneurs to understand their businesses better, and to be aware of the potential pitfalls before they start. Ask students to suggest some examples of strengths and weaknesses for businesses they know.

Discuss:

- What is a strength of the fast food chain McDonald's?

- What may be a weakness for someone wanting to start a local beautician and hairdresser?

- What is an example of a threat for a business?

- What might be an example of an opportunity for a new catering company?

EXPLORE

Place students into small groups and provide each group with a large sheet of paper and some marker pens. Ask each group to split their sheet into four boxes with one horizontal and one vertical line. In each box they should write the headings Strengths; Weaknesses; Opportunities; Threats.

Each group should conduct a SWOT analysis for a new business that wishes to set up in their local community area, writing their ideas within each box on their sheet of paper.

THEME 7: BUSINESS BASICS

Provide the following options, telling students to imagine the following companies have not yet opened their doors to the public, but are creating their business plans to try to get a bank loan to get them started:

- a hairdressing salon
- a pet shop
- a childminding service
- a catering company specialising in weddings.

TAKE IT FORWARD

Ask each group to share their SWOT analysis, providing some information about the company they chose to analyse.
Discuss:

- After completing the SWOT analysis, would you recommend the bank gives the business a loan to get them started?
- Why is it important for a business to conduct a SWOT analysis?
- Imagine you used the SWOT analysis on yourself. What might it say?

Activity 5: Profit and Loss
BUSINESS BASICS

> **Learning objectives** *To explore business budgeting*
> *To practise completing a business budget*
> *To analyse the profitability of a business*
>
> **Resources required** *Resource 7.6: Business Budget*

SET THE SCENE

Explain to students that an important part of business planning (and general life planning) is to keep track of finances by having a budget. A business budget keeps track of how much money will be coming in to the business in the form of sales, grants, investments and so forth, and how much money will be going out, to pay staff, pay for equipment or materials, pay for services the business needs, and so forth.

Ask students to briefly discuss some examples of the ways in which money might go out of a business (i.e. expenditure). What do businesses have to pay for?

Discuss briefly the ways businesses can make money. How can a business generate an income?

EXPLORE

Working in pairs or threes, give each group a copy of *Resource 7.6*. Students should review the business example and complete the budget spreadsheet, listing all the outgoings and income of the business in the appropriate columns. Students should use the following equation to determine whether the business will make a profit or loss:

Income − Expenditure = Profit (Loss)

TAKE IT FORWARD

Ask students to share their findings.

Discuss:

- How much profit or loss will the business make?
- Is the business viable, i.e. will it make enough profit to survive?
- Why is it useful to create a budget for a business?

THEME 7: BUSINESS BASICS

Activity 6: The Branding Game
BUSINESS BASICS

> **Learning objectives**   *To define the term 'branding'*
> *To explore why a business creates a brand*
> *To identify the successful attributes of a business's brand*
>
> **Resources required**   *Plain paper; marker pens; access to the Internet*

SET THE SCENE

Ask students to suggest what is meant by the term 'branding'. Why do companies want to create a recognised brand?

Branding is the process of marketing a business, product or service by creating a name, symbol or design to identify and differentiate it from its competitors. Often this is achieved with a logo, but also with slogans and catchphrases, colour schemes, and a 'message' or idea behind a product or business.

Ask students to suggest ideas for what they know of the branding for the following companies:

- Nike
- Starbucks
- McDonald's
- Apple.

Discuss:

- What colours are associated with each brand?

- What messages or ideas are each brand promoting, i.e. what does the brand want you to believe about their product?

- Why do people buy the product(s)? Is it really better than its competitors or are the customers buying into an idea the brand is selling, such as the idea that they are cool or fashionable if they buy the product?

ACTIVITY 6: THE BRANDING GAME

EXPLORE

Ask students to search for a number of logos from popular companies online, if they have access to the Internet at home, and discuss which logos they like the most and why.

Alternatively, ask students to create a logo for a fictitious brand. They should consider which colours, designs, text and layout to use.

TAKE IT FORWARD

Discuss:

- What do you notice about the logos?
- Which ones do you like the most and why? Which ones do you least like and why?
- Why do you think people recognise these logos so easily? How often do you see them and where?

Resource 7.1
Entrepreneur Case Study

Mike runs his own business, Odd Jobs. Mike used to work in construction, and has many qualifications – he knows how to do lots of jobs including plumbing, decorating, plastering, fixing electrics and rewiring. He has many years of experience and has taught others how to do these jobs, too. When Mike was made redundant from his last job he decided to set up his own business and market his skills locally, helping people with odd jobs in their homes.

Mike realised that there was a gap in the market – lots of people were too busy to do jobs that needed doing in their homes, or didn't have the skills to do them. He created a slogan for his business – 'We Do the Jobs You Don't Want To' – and promoted his business as a one-stop shop for all sorts of different household problems. He found that many customers would request his help with one thing, but that would lead to lots of other work when they realised he did such a good job.

Mike advertised locally and gained some customers. He worked quickly and efficiently and was always friendly. He charged reasonable prices, and gained a good reputation in his area. Mike took on a young man to be his assistant and trained him up while they worked. As more and more work came in, Mike helped his assistant to become more confident and to gain qualifications to allow him to do jobs on his own. Mike found a business advisor to help him create a detailed business plan, with a budget and cashflow projections to work out how much money he would spend and how much profit he would make each year. Before long, Mike had employed another two members of staff. He took out a bank loan and bought a van, and then a second.

After two years Mike rented a small office and employed an administrator to take over all the paperwork and office duties, including answering phone calls from customers, sending invoices and paying bills. After five years Mike decided to franchise the business (sell the brand of the business on a licence, so someone would pay him a fee to run Odd Jobs in their town). Mike sold franchises to three people in different parts of the country, and helped them to get started. He stopped doing the hands-on work for customers and instead managed the team and the franchisees.

Within ten years Mike had a thriving business with Odd Jobs franchises up and down the country. Mike sold the whole business for over £5 million and retired at the age of 50.

After reading the case study, discuss the following in your group.

- Why do people become entrepreneurs?
- Having a good initial idea is important, but what keeps people in business and successful in the long term?
- What skills do entrepreneurs possess?
- What kind of attitude or mindset does an entrepreneur need?

Resource 7.2
Entrepreneur Profile

Think of a famous entrepreneur and research them online to learn more about how they got started and became successful.

NAME OF ENTREPRENEUR: _____

- How did they get started as an entrepreneur?
- What challenges did the entrepreneur face?
- What did they have to do to become the successful entrepreneur they are today?
- What do you admire about this person?
- What qualities do you think they possess?

Resource 7.3
Budget Planner

Use the budget planner below to calculate the cost of building your house. Next, decide how much you will charge for your house, and calculate whether you've made a profit, or loss (Sale price – Costs = Profit/Loss).

- Cardboard – £2.00
- Paper – £1.00
- Scissors – £0.50 per pair
- Glue – £1.00 per stick
- Sticky tape – £5.00 per roll
- Paperclips – £0.10 per paperclip
- Marker pens – £0.30 per pen
- Straws/sticks – £0.25 per straw/stick
- Coloured card – £0.50

Item purchased	Quantity	Cost (£)

Total cost of items purchased: _____

Your selling price: _____

Profit/Loss: _____

Resource 7.4
Business Jargon

Advertising: A method of communication to promote what the business is selling, to raise awareness and gain more sales.

Branding: The design, symbol and 'look' of a business to help people recognise it and sell products or services.

Business plan: A document outlining the plans for the business which can be used to gain funding or investment.

Capital: The resources needed to start or run the business, e.g. buildings, equipment or tools, or the money used to purchase these items.

Cash flow: The amount of money moving (flowing) in and out of the business each month.

Demand: The desire for the product or service.

Entrepreneur: An individual who starts, grows and manages the business.

Founder: The person who started the business originally.

Investment: Money or other resources put into the business to get it started, keep it running or to grow the business.

Marketing: Methods to promote the business to gain more customers.

Mission statement: A simple sentence or sentences which sum up what the business aims to do.

Profit: The amount of money that is left after all the expenses of running a business have been deducted from the income.

Public relations: The process of communicating what a business does or stands for to its customers and potential customers, e.g. through the media.

Sales forecast: A process and document to estimate a business's future sales to enable the company to make informed business decisions and predict sales on a short-term and long-term basis.

Slogan: A catchy phrase to help customers remember the business and what it sells.

Start-up: A business in the early stages of growth.

Trademark: A symbol, word or phrase legally registered by a company to represent their brand, service or product.

Resource 7.5
Business Case Study

BELLA'S BEAUTY SALON

Bella's Beauty Salon is a small shop in the centre of Knowlesville. Bella's Beauty Salon provides a range of beauty services, including manicures, make-up, massages, hairdressing, spray tans and much more. Bella's Salon aims to 'Help you to feel beautiful inside and out'.

Knowlesville is a growing town, and a local celebrity has moved into the area. She is often being photographed wearing the latest fashions and looking glamorous. This is encouraging lots of other local women to want to look their best to be like the celeb. Bella's Beauty Salon has approached the celebrity to be its 'brand ambassador' – talking about Bella's and promoting the business online in exchange for free services.

Bella's Beauty Salon has a website, and Facebook and Instagram accounts, where it shares photos of clients' hairstyles, makeovers and nails, with their permission. Bella's Beauty Salon is very popular with women aged 18–40, but the owner realises that they could increase their business with younger clients by offering pamper parties to children and teens.

There are lots of other similar businesses in the area, and Bella's Beauty Salon needs to make sure it offers something different, or it may lose its customers and go out of business quickly.

- What is the company's mission? (i.e. what does it intend to do? Why is it in business?)

- How will the business make money? (i.e. what are its main products or services?)

- Who are its main customers?

- How will the owner market their business? (i.e. how will they let their customers know what Bella's Beauty Salon has to offer?)

- Does this business have the potential to be successful, or not?

Resource 7.6
Business Budget

JIM'S GOURMET POPCORN

Jim runs a business selling gourmet popcorn. He rents an office with a kitchen where he makes the popcorn, which costs him £250 per month including his electricity and water bills. Jim makes popcorn to sell to local shops, and sells his popcorn directly to customers at festivals and fayres during the Christmas period and the summer. Jim sells £500-worth of popcorn to local shops each month on fixed agreements with the shops.

In December Jim sells a lot of popcorn at Christmas fayres and local festivals. He sells each box of popcorn for £3 and in December he sells 150 boxes. In April he sells 85 boxes at Easter time, and in May he sells another 25 boxes at a local film festival.

Jim has to pay insurance each month on his equipment and to cover himself in case anyone were to become ill after eating his popcorn. This costs him £25 per month.

Jim has a business bank account which costs him £5 a month in fees. He has two members of staff who each work for £6 per hour, and work 30 hours per week.

Jim's telephone bill varies, depending on how much he uses it. In busy months such as December, April and May his phone bill is £30 per month. In quiet months it is £15.

Jim designs flyers in December to promote his popcorn, which cost him £50 to be printed. In January it is so quiet that Jim decides to post a flyer to every household in his local area (1,000 homes) which costs him £0.30 per flyer in postage. At other times, Jim's postage costs are minimal, at £5 per month.

In March Jim pays to advertise his business on Facebook which costs him £15.

Jim drives around to drop off the popcorn to the local shops that he supplies. It costs him £40 to fill up his tank with petrol and he uses a whole tank each month to get around to every shop. When Jim goes to local festivals and fairs (December, April and May) he uses an additional £10 of petrol each month.

Jim pays £0.20 for each bucket he uses to put the popcorn in. Jim pays £0.50 per box for the actual popcorn. He then adds flavourings which cost an additional £0.20 per box of popcorn.

Is Jim's business profitable, or not? Use the budget template on the next page and work out Jim's sales (income) and his expenditure, to calculate his profit or loss.

Jim's Gourmet Popcorn Business Budget

Income	(£) Month 1	(£) Month 2	(£) Month 3	(£) Month 4	(£) Month 5	(£) Month 6
Sales						

Expenditure – fixed	(£) Month 1	(£) Month 2	(£) Month 3	(£) Month 4	(£) Month 5	(£) Month 6
Office rent and bills						
Insurance						
Bank fees						
Staff wages						

Expenditure – variable	(£) Month 1	(£) Month 2	(£) Month 3	(£) Month 4	(£) Month 5	(£) Month 6
Telephone bill						
Postage						
Advertising costs						
Travel costs						
Popcorn						
Flavourings						
Popcorn buckets						
TOTAL						

Overall income for 6 months: _____

Overall expenditure for 6 months: _____

Profit (Loss): Income – Expenditure = Profit (Loss) _____

Theme 8

Ignition

The final theme, Ignition, helps young people to assimilate their learning throughout the whole programme and take positive, concrete steps towards their future. Activities in Theme 8 help young people to ignite their passions and desires and set goals, and create the mindset needed to achieve their dreams.

Learning objectives

By the end of this module, students will:

- create clear, concrete steps towards their future goals and success
- define and articulate their personal vision of success
- identify their personal power, control and choice to create their future visions
- develop practical ways to take next steps.

Activities

- Being a Successful Person
- Who Is Successful?
- Universal versus Personal Success
- The Power Circle
- Personal Power
- Self-Talk
- I Believe in You!
- Self-Discovery
- Sell Yourself
- Personal Mission Statement.

To conclude or extend the RfL programme, you may wish to consider furthering young people's learning journeys outside of the classroom by organising trips or experiences that will contextualise the knowledge gained, such as:

- organising visits to local businesses or universities
- arranging short-term work experience opportunities
- encouraging and supporting young people to access volunteering opportunities
- arranging visits to local inspirational role models
- exploring the possibility of accrediting young people's learning through vocational learning centres so participants gain a recognised qualification, for example in entrepreneurship.

THEME 8: IGNITION

Activity 1: Being a Successful Person
IGNITION

> **Learning objectives** *To define and understand the concept of success*
> *To explore the difference between universal or stereotypical ideas of success and personal measures of success*
>
> **Resources required** *Large sheet of paper and/or whiteboard; sticky notes; marker pens; Resource 8.1: The Successful Man; Resource 8.2: The Successful Man Revealed*

SET THE SCENE

Ask students the meaning of the word 'success' and discuss:

- What is success?
- What does it mean to be successful?
- Who do you consider to be a successful person? Why?
- What are some words you might use to describe a successful person? (Note these on the board or on a large sheet of paper to refer back to.)
- How does someone become successful?

EXPLORE

Display the photograph in *Resource 8.1* using a projector or print copies for students to study. Ask students to list their immediate thoughts and reactions to the person in the picture on paper or sticky notes, sticking them on or near the image, or on the table in front of them, depending on the size of the group.

Discuss:

- What are your assumptions about the person?
- What do you think this man's life is like?
- What might be this man's story? What does he do for a living? Where might he live? What does he do in his spare time?
- What words might you use to describe this man?

Give students some time to write their ideas and come back together as a whole group and share answers. Now, present the students with the information about the man in

ACTIVITY 1: BEING A SUCCESSFUL PERSON

Resource 8.2. Ask whether their ideas and assumptions about the man have changed. Do they still consider him to be successful?

TAKE IT FORWARD

Ask students to share what this exercise tells us about success. Is it as simple as it seems?

THEME 8: IGNITION

Activity 2: Who Is Successful?

IGNITION

> **Learning objectives** *To define and understand the concept of success*
> *To identify stereotypes and assumptions about success*
> *To begin to define students' own ideas about success, and the skills and competencies they already possess to create personal success*
>
> **Resources required** *Resource 8.3: Success Profiles*

SET THE SCENE

Ask students to consider what success means to them.

Is there one definition of success, or does it depend on the individual? Do ideas about success differ from country to country, and might they change over time?

Explain to students that they will look at two examples of very different people, and discuss whether they perceive them to be successful, or not.

EXPLORE

Split students into groups of three to four and give each group a set of *Resource 8.3: Success Profiles*.

Ask the groups to read the profiles and decide whether each person is 'a success' or not. Students must be able to explain and justify their answer, so they should take some time to consider what makes the person a success – there are no right or wrong answers, however, just their opinions.

Come back together as a whole group and discuss each profile and their answers.

TAKE IT FORWARD

Discuss:

- Did this activity change anyone's ideas about success?

- How did this activity make you think about your own success? Are you a successful person?

Activity 3: Universal versus Personal Success
IGNITION

> **Learning objectives**   *To define and understand the concept of success*
> *To explore the difference between universal or stereotypical ideas of success and personal measures of success*
> *To identify stereotypes and assumptions about success*
> *To begin to define students' own ideas about success, and the skills and competencies they already possess to create personal success*
>
> **Resources required**   *Large sheets of paper; marker pens*

SET THE SCENE

Explain to students that this activity will help them to explore more about their own personal definitions of success. Although we might have ideas about success in terms of jobs and careers, being successful can also mean we do certain things or have a certain mindset in our personal life.

EXPLORE

Split students into groups of approximately four to six people. Give each group a large sheet of paper and some marker pens. Ask each group to discuss and brainstorm either:

- What it means to be successful in your career/job

    or

- What it means to be a successful person.

You may wish to mention that some of the groups' answers might be similar or the same, but there may be some differences, too. For example, someone might be very successful at work, but lack success in other areas of their life, or vice versa. You may wish to spend some time discussing this, to ensure students fully understand.

Come back together and discuss each group's answers and ideas. Are there any differences between being successful at work and being a generally successful person?

THEME 8: IGNITION

TAKE IT FORWARD

Discuss:

- Did the activity surprise you in any way?

- Which matters more, being successful in your work or being a successful person? Are they interlinked?

- Can someone be both?

Activity 4: The Power Circle
IGNITION

> **Learning objectives** *To explore the concepts of personal power and control*
> *To define and understand the concept of 'locus of control'*
> *To encourage students to explore ways in which they can feel empowered about their future*
>
> **Resources required** *A selection of soft balls*

SET THE SCENE

Introduce the main themes for this RfL activity: power and control. You may wish to refer back to Theme 1, Activity 4, which explores the concept of a locus of control. Explain to students that a person's locus of control is a phrase which means how much people believe that they can control events that affect them. A person's 'locus' can either be internal (the person believes they can control their life) or external (meaning they believe that their decisions and life are controlled by factors which they cannot influence, or by chance or fate). Ask students to share their thoughts on the following discussion points:

- Who has control over your life?

- What does it mean to be in control of your life? What might this look and feel like?

- As young people, there are some parts of your life that you don't have much control over, like whether you can choose to go to school or not, or where you live, for example. What *do* you have control over?

EXPLORE

Explain to students that they will be playing a game to explore the concepts of power and control. Ask students to gather in a circle, standing fairly close to one another. Ask for a volunteer to be the leader of the game. This person will be the 'Powerful One'. They have power over everyone else, and can control how they play the game.

Introduce four balls into the circle. Ideally these balls should be of varying sizes and shapes, but should be soft to avoid anyone getting hurt. The balls must be thrown to each person in the circle in a sequence without dropping them, starting and ending with the Powerful One.

Starting with just one ball, the Powerful One should throw it to someone else in the circle, saying their name. They should then in turn throw the ball to someone else, saying *their* name. This should be repeated until everyone has had a go and the ball has returned back to the Powerful One. Students should remember the sequence in which they received and threw the ball as they will repeat this pattern over and over.

THEME 8: IGNITION

Once everyone has remembered the sequence, the game can begin again. The Powerful One can add in more balls at any time, starting the sequence over, and can also exert their power over other players by making the game more difficult for them. The Powerful One can point to anyone at any time and say:

- use one hand
- go down on one knee
- go down on both knees
- close one eye
- turn around and look over your shoulder to play.

They can cancel this order at any time too, by pointing to the person and saying 'cancel'. It is up to the Powerful One how many people he or she chooses to control!

TAKE IT FORWARD

After a few minutes, end the game and come back together as a full group.
Discuss:

- How did it feel to be the Powerful One?
- How did it feel to be controlled by the Powerful One?
- This game was just a bit of fun, but it helped us to explore the idea of having power over others or being disempowered. How does it feel when we have no control or power in our lives?

Activity 5: Personal Power
IGNITION

> **Learning objectives**   *To define and understand the concept of personal power*
> *To explore the aspects of life we have control over*
> *To explore the impact of a lack of control and power, and define alternative, positive ways to meet our needs for power*
>
> **Resources required**   *Large sheets of paper; marker pens*

SET THE SCENE

Introduce the concept of having lots of power and control over some parts of our lives, and less over other parts of our lives. Sometimes people can struggle with a feeling of a lack of control, or may seek alternative ways to feel independent, powerful and in control, which might be positive or negative.

EXPLORE

Split students into groups of approximately four to six and give each group a large sheet of paper and some marker pens. Each group should draw a line down the centre of their paper and write the following headings on each side: 'I can control…' and 'I have to live with…'. Each group should spend a few minutes brainstorming the things in their lives they can control and have power over, and the things they cannot control and must live with.

Come back together as a whole group and ask each group to share their ideas.

TAKE IT FORWARD

Discuss:

- How does it feel to have control over those parts of our lives?

- How does it feel to not have any power or control over some parts of our lives?

- Although we can't always control these parts of life, we *can* control how we respond to them, including our thoughts, feelings and actions. Can anyone think of a way in which they can respond to one of those parts of life they have to live with?

- How can we change our thoughts to change our experience of life or people in our life?

THEME 8: IGNITION

Activity 6: Self-Talk
IGNITION

> **Learning objectives** *To explore the concept of self-talk and our inner critic*
> *To acknowledge the role of our inner voice and notice negative self-talk*
> *To reframe a negative inner voice to a more positive and affirming voice*
> *To explore the impact of a negative inner voice on our feelings and behaviours*
>
> **Resources required** *Resource 5.2: Speech Bubbles (photocopied and cut up, enough for 3–4 per person); marker pens; sticky tack; sticky notes*

SET THE SCENE

Ask students to suggest some ideas about what 'self-talk' might mean.

Self-talk relates to the voice within our heads that chatters away all day. Our self-talk can be fairly ordinary, like thinking about what we'll have for lunch. Sometimes our self-talk is positive, congratulating us for doing a good job or reassuring us that we did something right. At other times our self-talk can be very negative or critical, such as thoughts of being left out by our friends, or telling us we're not good at a certain school subject.

Sometimes we notice our thoughts, and if they are negative and critical, we can choose to think better thoughts. However, sometimes the voice in our mind chatters away non-stop and we believe everything it says, even if it isn't nice, and we feel powerless to change it.

EXPLORE

Explain to the group the importance of listening to our inner voice, and training ourselves to challenge negative thoughts so we can create healthy self-talk, which creates positive feelings and behaviours.

Place the cut-out speech bubbles from *Resource 5.2* and some marker pens in the middle of the circle and ask students to write some examples of their self-talk in the following scenarios:

- What is your inner voice saying when you are...trying something new at school?
- What is your inner voice saying when you are...about to take a test?

ACTIVITY 6: SELF-TALK

- What is your inner voice saying when you are...with someone you've never met before?
- What is your inner voice saying when you are...thinking about your future?

Allow some time for the students to complete their speech bubbles, encouraging them to be as honest as possible. Their answers can be anonymous – they do not need to add their name.

Each student should now re-read their bubbles, deciding if their self-talk is positive or negative. When everyone is ready, ask the students to tack any negative speech bubbles to a large wall in the room.

Explain to the group that they should now think of examples of positive self-talk that can balance the negative self-talk in the speech bubbles on the wall. They should write down as many examples as they can think of using sticky notes, and tack them on the wall around each speech bubble. They can choose to write as many positive comments as they can, for their and other people's speech bubbles.

TAKE IT FORWARD

Discuss:

- Was anyone surprised by their self-talk?
- What are the consequences of having a negative inner voice?
- What are the consequences of having a positive inner voice?
- Does anyone's inner voice sound like someone they know? How does it feel to hear it?
- How can we change our self-talk from negative to positive?
- Where did these thoughts come from? When did they start?

THEME 8: IGNITION

Activity 7: I Believe in You!
IGNITION

> **Learning objectives** *To explore the concept of self-belief*
> *To demonstrate positive regard for others*
> *To acknowledge our own strengths, gifts and worth*
>
> **Resources required** *Plain paper; marker pens; masking tape*

SET THE SCENE

Remind students about the importance of self-belief – believing and trusting in our positive qualities, and having self-confidence and self-worth.

Ask students to share one way in which they have demonstrated self-belief this week.

EXPLORE

Give each student a piece of plain paper and a marker pen, and ask the group to help one another to tape the paper to each other's back, using masking tape.

When everyone has a sheet of paper on their back, explain to the group that they must spend a few minutes writing a comment on each person's back to share why they believe in that person. For example, 'I believe in you because you are determined'. Ask the group to consider what skills, talents and attributes each person holds that will help them to be successful in life.

Each comment should be written anonymously, and students should try to write a comment on everyone's paper. Stress the importance of no negative or disrespectful comments, even in jest.

After ten minutes or so, bring the group back together and allow each person to untape their paper and read the comments.

TAKE IT FORWARD

Discuss:

- How does it feel to read those comments?

- Was anyone surprised by a comment someone wrote?

- How does it feel to have people believing in us? How can this help us to reach our goals and dreams?

Activity 8: Self-Discovery
IGNITION

> **Learning objectives** *To explore the importance of acknowledging our strengths, talents and positive attributes*
> *To define and share our strengths and positive qualities*
> *To explore how to present ourselves positively to others, such as when applying for a job or college course*
>
> **Resources required** *Resource 8.4: Self-Discovery Worksheet*

SET THE SCENE

Explain to students how important it is for us to get to know our strengths, talents and positive qualities when we come to apply for college, university or a job. We must present ourselves in the best possible light, helping people to understand what we have to give to the organisation or company. We each have something unique to offer.

Sometimes we sell ourselves short, or we fail to see all the positive things other people see in us.

EXPLORE

Give each student a copy of *Resource 8.4: Self-Discovery Worksheet*. They should work individually to answer each question, taking time to reflect upon their thoughts and feelings as they complete the worksheet. Some of the questions might be a little difficult, but they can ask another group member for their opinions.

Come back together as a whole group and discuss answers, if they feel comfortable doing so.

TAKE IT FORWARD

Discuss:

- How might this worksheet help us to write a CV or apply for a volunteering position, for example?

- Which answers are you most proud of and why?

- We are often taught from a young age that talking about our talents and achievements is 'boasting' and arrogant. People often talk about their shortcomings and failures, but rarely their successes. What might be the consequence of this?

THEME 8: IGNITION

Activity 9: Sell Yourself
IGNITION

> **Learning objectives** *To explore the concept of positive self-promotion*
> *To explore ways to share our positive attributes, skills or achievements with others*
> *To practise presentation skills and public speaking*
>
> **Resources required** *Plain paper; drawing materials*

SET THE SCENE

Ask students to suggest ideas about what makes us like someone. What attracts us to some people so we want to spend time with them, be their friend, etc., such as their appearance, personality, friendliness, honesty, shared problems, things in common, etc.?

Explain to students that when we are applying for college, a volunteer position, apprenticeship or job we must sell ourselves, both on paper and in person. Someone who has never met us before will not know anything about the kind of person we are, the good things we have done in the past, the experience we have, our hobbies and interests or our goals and dreams. But all of this information is almost useless if we can't communicate it clearly!

Selling ourselves is linked to presentation skills, making a good first impression and excelling at interviews, all of which have been explored in Skills for Life.

EXPLORE

Provide each student with a blank sheet of paper and some drawing materials. Explain to the group that they must create an advert to sell themselves, as if they were an advert in a magazine! You may wish to provide students with some examples of advertisements to provide inspiration.

Students should consider what an employer might want to see – they can use images and words.

Ask students to present their adverts. Ask the rest of the group to consider if each advert is clear, and if they understand what the person has to offer.

TAKE IT FORWARD

Discuss:

- Was it difficult to 'sell yourself' on paper? Some people can find this challenging as it feels boastful or arrogant to talk about their attributes, while other people struggle to find anything positive to say about themselves.

- How can you 'sell' your skills and experience in real life?

- Why is it important to 'sell' yourself when you are looking for education, training or employment opportunities?

THEME 8: IGNITION

Activity 10: Personal Mission Statement
IGNITION

> **Learning objectives** *To define and understand the term 'mission statement'*
> *To create a personal mission statement*
> *To explore and communicate aspects of our identity, values, goals and strengths*
>
> **Resources required** *Plain paper and/or whiteboard; marker pens*

SET THE SCENE

Ask students if anyone remembers the definition of what a 'mission statement' is from *Resource 7.4: Business Jargon*. Has anyone read a mission statement before?

A mission statement is a short sentence or paragraph explaining what a company or organisation aims to do. It outlines the company's mission and goals, why they are in operation and how the company aims to function.

Ask students what a personal mission statement might include if they were creating a mission statement for themselves.

EXPLORE

Students will create their own personal mission statement in this activity, explaining in a short sentence or paragraph:

- Who they are
- Who they want to be/their goals
- What they stand for.

Their mission statement should help them to explain who they are to other people, and can be used on job or college application forms, on their CV and in interviews.

Give each student a blank piece of paper and ask them to craft their personal mission statement. Display the following questions on the whiteboard or on a large sheet of paper, to help students if needed.

1. What is my life about – what is my life's purpose? (e.g. your identity; who you are)
2. What do I stand for? (e.g. your values and beliefs)
3. What accomplishments am I working towards? (e.g. your goals)

TAKE IT FORWARD

Ask each student to share their personal mission statement. Discuss how they can use this statement in practical ways, and to help keep them on track with their goals.

Resource 8.1
The Successful Man

Resource 8.2
The Successful Man Revealed

> This man is £35,000 in debt.

> This man hasn't had a holiday in four years. He is hoping to retire at 50 though.

> This man is divorced and currently lives alone. He does not see his two children.

> This man was fired from his last job for stealing from the company.

> This man currently works 60 hours a week. He does not have time for hobbies.

Resource 8.3
Success Profiles

Janet is 55 years old and works part time on the checkout at a local grocery store for minimum wage. She has two grown-up children and four grandchildren. Janet is passionate about helping people and volunteers at a local nursing home with dementia patients, and at a local animal shelter as she loves dogs.

Because she works part time, Janet is able to care for her young grandchildren and picks them up from school each day to take them to the park and feed them dinner. This also means her daughter can work full time, as she wouldn't be able to afford childcare on her salary.

Janet loves to visit new places and saves up to go on one big holiday each year. So far she's travelled to the USA, Australia, India and New Zealand with her husband. She looks forward to researching and planning the trip all year long.

Because Janet has lots of free time she sees her friends often, and is part of a number of local groups and clubs, including an art class and book club.

Paul is 40 and works for a private bank in London as a financial analyst. His job is very important and he is under a lot of pressure to make money for the bank. Paul typically works 60–80 hours per week and usually gets to the office for 7am and leaves after 7pm. He has a wife and two young children who live on the outskirts of London in a large house with a swimming pool. It takes Paul an hour to commute each way, so he leaves home early in the morning and doesn't get back until late, when the children are usually in bed.

Paul earns over £200,000 a year. He has a very large mortgage on his home, and has to pay for two luxury cars. His wife does not work and likes to go shopping for designer clothes and furniture. Paul and his wife typically go on three or four luxury holidays each year but Paul usually has to work while he's away, especially if there's a crisis at the office.

Paul has been under a lot of stress recently and is suffering from chest pains. He is overweight as he doesn't have time to exercise, and is worried he might have a heart attack because of his poor diet.

Resource 8.4
Self-Discovery Worksheet

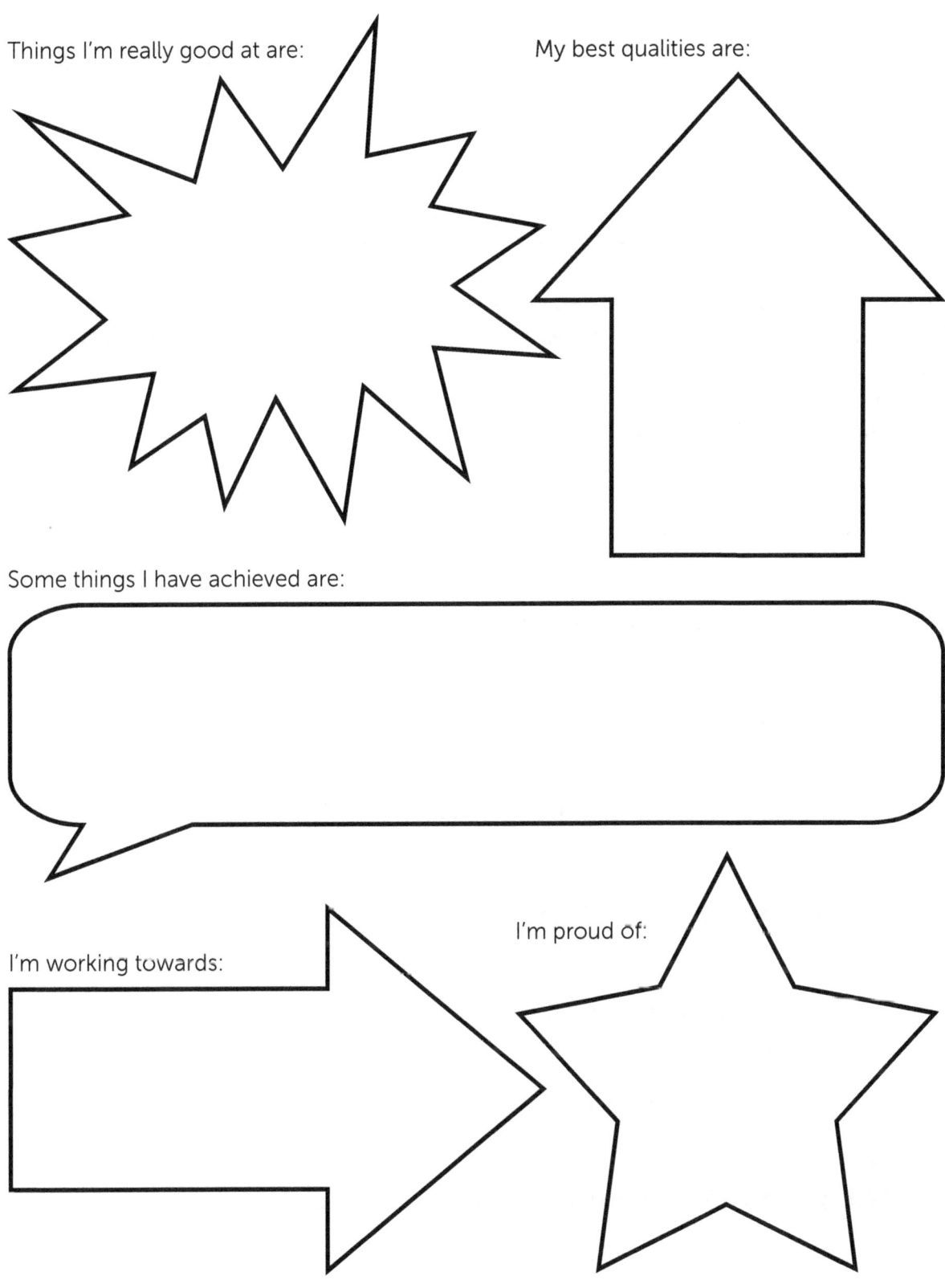

Appendix 1

RfL Assessment Tool

Name: _____ **Class:** _____

Read the questions below and decide whether you agree, disagree or don't know. There are no right or wrong answers, just your opinion. Try to be as honest as you can.

1. I have goals for the future.

    Agree   Disagree   Maybe/Don't Know

2. I know what I want to do when I leave school.

    Agree   Disagree   Maybe/Don't Know

3. I believe I have what it takes to be successful.

    Agree   Disagree   Maybe/Don't Know

4. I feel excited about the future.

    Agree   Disagree   Maybe/Don't Know

5. I feel prepared for my next steps in life.

    Agree   Disagree   Maybe/Don't Know

6. I think that having a good education is important.

    Agree Disagree Maybe/Don't Know

7. I am in control of my life and my future.

    Agree Disagree Maybe/Don't Know

8. I know where to go to get help with making decisions about my future.

    Agree Disagree Maybe/Don't Know

9. I plan on going to university or undertaking further study after I leave school.

    Agree Disagree Maybe/Don't Know

10. I have something unique to offer the world.

    Agree Disagree Maybe/Don't Know

11. I am a successful person.

    Agree Disagree Maybe/Don't Know

12. I am capable of achieving whatever I desire.

    Agree Disagree Maybe/Don't Know

Thank you!

Appendix 2

Certificate of Achievement

Readiness for Life

Supporting School Engagement, Aspirations and Success in Young People

This is to certify that

_____

has taken part in a year long programme, exploring enterprise skills, career development and financial literacy to build aspirations, motivation to learn, and school engagement.

Signed _____ Dated _____

References

Ariely, D., Gneezy, U., Loewenstein, G. and Mazar, N. (2009) 'Large stakes and big mistakes'. *Review of Economic Studies*, 76, 451–469.

Bhavnani, R. (2006) *Ahead of the Game: The Changing Aspirations of Young Ethnic Minority Women*. Manchester: Equal Opportunities Commission.

Bourdieu, P. (1973) *Cultural Reproduction and Social Reproduction in Knowledge, Education and Cultural Change*. London: Tavistock.

Bradley, S. and Taylor, J. (2004) 'Ethnicity, educational attainment and the transition from school.' *The Manchester School*, 72(3), 317–346.

Broecke, S. and Nicholls, T. (2006) *Ethnicity and Degree Attainment*. London: Department for Education and Skills.

Bureau of Labor Statistics (2017) *Employment and Unemployment Among Youth Summary*. Washington, DC: United States Department of Labor. Accessed on 31/05/18 at www.bls.gov/news.release/youth.nr0.htm

Cabinet Office (2008) *Achieving Culture Change: A Policy Framework*. London: Cabinet Office Strategy Unit.

Crawford, C. and Greaves, E. (2015) *Socio-Economic, Ethnic and Gender Differences in HE Participation*. BIS Research Paper No. 186. Accessed on 29/08/17 at www.gov.uk/government/publications/higher-education-participation-socio-economic-ethnic-and-gender-differences

Deci, E. (1971) 'Effects of Externally Mediated Rewards on Intrinsic Motivation.' *Journal of Personality and Social Psychology*, 18(1) 105–115.

Department for Business, Innovation and Skills (2013) *Motivation and Barriers to Learning for Young People not in Education, Employment or Training*. London: Department for Business, Innovation and Skills.

Department for Children, Schools and Families (DCSF) (2008) *Aspiration and Attainment Amongst Young People In Deprived Communities*. London: Cabinet Office.

Department for Education (2017) *Schools, Pupils and Their Characteristics: January 2017*. London: Department for Education.

Eccles, J., Midgley, C., Wigfield, A., Reuman, D., Mac Iver, D. and Feldlaufer, H. (1993) 'Negative effects of traditional middle schools on students' motivation'. *Elementary School Journal*, 93, 553–574.

Estyn (2018) *Common Inspection Framework*. Cardiff: Estyn. Accessed on 16/12/18 at https://www.estyn.gov.wales/inspection/inspection-explained/common-inspection-framework

Fawcett Society (2017) *Gender Pay Gap and Causes Briefing*. London: Fawcett Society. Accessed on 30/05/18 at www.fawcettsociety.org.uk/equal-pay-day-2017-briefing

Fawcett Society (2018) 'No Safety Net for UK's Worst Paid Women'. London: Fawcett Society. Accessed on 30/05/18 at www.fawcettsociety.org.uk/news/no-safety-net-for-uks-worst-paid-women

Feinstein, L., Duckworth, K. and Sabates, R. (2004) *A Model of the Intergenerational Transmission of Educational Success*. London: Centre for the Wider Benefits of Learning, Institute of Education, University of London.

Guardian (2017) 'University gender gap at record high as 30,000 more women accepted'. London: Guardian News and Media Limited. Accessed on 29/08/17 at www.theguardian.com/education/2017/aug/28/university-gender-gap-at-record-high-as-30000-more-women-accepted

Gutman, L. and Akerman, R. (2008) *Determinants of Aspirations*. London: Centre for Research on the Wider Benefits of Learning, Institute of Education, University of London.

Hargreaves, A. and Fullan, M. (2013) *Professional Capital: Transforming Teaching in Every School*. Ashland, OR: Blackstone Audio, Inc.

LearnDirect (2011) 'Debt Facts and Figures – Compiled April 2011.' *Credit Action*. Accessed on 30/05/2018 at https://themoneycharity.org.uk/media/april-2011.pdf

Lewis, G., Gewirtz, S. and Clarke, J. (eds) (2000) *Rethinking Social Policy*. London: Open University.

Lupton, R. (2006) 'How does place affect education?' In S. Delorenzi (ed.) *Going Places: Neighbourhood, Ethnicity and Social Mobility*. London: IPPR.

Lupton, R. and Kintrea, K. (2011) 'Can community-based interventions on aspirations raise young people's attainment?' *Social Policy and Society*, 10(3), 321–335.

Maslow, A. (1943) 'A Theory of Human Motivation.' *Psychological Review*, 50, 370–396.

Modood, T., Berthoud, R., Lakey, J., Nazroo, J. *et al.* (1997) *Ethnic Minorities in Britain: Diversity and Disadvantage*. London: Policy Studies Institute.

Moneysaving Expert (2017) 'Are your savings safe?' Accessed on 30/11/17 at www.moneysavingexpert.com/savings/safe-savings

MORI/Sutton Trust (2006) *Creating a High Aspiration Culture for Young People in the UK*. London: The Sutton Trust.

Northwest Regional Development Agency (NWDA) (2010) *Raising the Aspirations and Attainment Amongst Young People, Especially Amongst 16–19 Year Olds, and Stimulate an Interest in and Progression Towards Higher Skills*. Warrington, UK: NWDA.

Ofsted (2011) *Girls' Career Aspirations*. London: Ofsted.

Oxford Living Dictionaries (2018) 'Definition of *aspiration* in English'. Oxford: Oxford University Press. Accessed on 30/05/18 at https://en.oxforddictionaries.com/definition/aspiration

Paton, G. (2013) 'School leavers "lacking basic skills", say business leaders'. *The Telegraph*, 14/08/13. Accessed on 15/06/2017 at www.telegraph.co.uk/education/universityeducation/clearing/10239980/School-leavers-lacking-basic-skills-say-business-leaders.html

Patten, E. and Parker, K. (2012) 'A gender reversal on career aspirations: Young women now top young men in valuing a high-paying career'. Washington, DC: Pew Research Center. Accessed on 09/06/17 at www.pewsocialtrends.org/2012/04/19/a-gender-reversal-on-career-aspirations

Pew Research Center (2018) *The Narrowing, but Persistent, Gender Gap in Pay*. Washington, DC: Pew Research Center.

Pink, D. (2011) *Drive: The Surprising Truth About What Motivates Us*. New York, NY: Riverhead Books.

Plewis, I. (2011) 'Contextual variations in ethnic group differences in educational attainments'. *Journal of the Royal Statistical Society Series A*, 174(2), 419–437.

Powell, A. (2018) *NEET: Young People Not in Education, Employment or Training*. London: House of Commons Library. Accessed on 07/07/17 at https://researchbriefings.parliament.uk/ResearchBriefing/Summary/SN06705#fullreport

Prince's Trust (2011) *Broke, Not Broken: Tackling Youth Poverty and the Aspiration Gap*. London: Prince's Trust.

Raphael-Reed, L., Gates, P. and Last, K. (2007) *Young Participation in Higher Education in the Parliamentary Constituencies of Birmingham Hodge Hill, Bristol South, Nottingham North and Sheffield Brightside*. Bristol: Higher Education Funding Council for England.

Strand, S. (2007) *Minority Ethnic Pupils in the Longitudinal Study of Young People in England (LSYPE)*. Warwick: University of Warwick.

Sullivan, A. (2001) 'Cultural Capital and Educational Attainment'. *Sociology*, 34(4), 893–912.

Sullivan, A. (2002) 'Bourdieu and education: How useful is Bourdieu's theory for researchers?' *Netherlands Journal of Social Sciences*, 38(2), 144–166.

The Money Advice Service (2018) 'Identity theft and scams: How to get your money back'. Accessed on 29/08/18 at www.moneyadviceservice.org.uk/en/articles/identity-theft-and-scams-what-you-are-liable-for

The Money Charity (2018a) *The Money Statistics January 2018*. London: The Money Charity. Accessed on 05/05/18 at https://themoneycharity.org.uk/media/January-2018-Money-Statistics.pdf

The Money Charity (2018b) *The Money Statistics March 2018*. London: The Money Charity. Accessed on 05/05/18 at https://themoneycharity.org.uk/media/March-2018-Money-Statistics.pdf

University of Oxford (2015) 'Study reveals careers "gender gap" for university graduates'. Accessed on 09/06/17 at www.ox.ac.uk/news/2015-01-13-study-reveals-careers-gender-gap-university-graduates

Vallerand, R., Blanchard, C., Mageau, G.A., Koestner, R. *et al.* (2003) 'Les passions de l'ame: On obsessive and harmonious passion'. *Journal of Personality and Social Psychology*, 85(4), 756–767.

Welsh Government (2015) *Quality and Effectiveness Framework*. Cardiff: Welsh Government. Accessed on 16/12/18 at https://beta.gov.wales/post-16-quality-and-data-management

Index

age
    and improvements in aspiration 31–2
Agree or Disagree? 106–7, 125–7
Akerman, R. 18
Are You a Team Player? 101, 118–19
Ariely, D. 40
aspiration improvement
    combining factors and approaches in 34–6
    cultural change in 32–4
    multi-faceted approach to 32
    skills change in 32–4
    starting age for 31–2
aspirations
    beliefs role in 25
    community role in 21–3
    definition of 17–18
    and ethnicity 29–30
    friends role in 19–20
    and gender 27–8
    media role in 20–1
    parental role in 19
    peer groups role in 19–20
    research on 18–24
    schools role in 20
    self-belief role in 23–5
    societal role in 20–1
    values role in 25
assessment of Readiness for Life sessions 64–5
    tools for 292–3

behaviour management in Readiness for Life sessions 62
Being Informed
    as pillar of Readiness for Life programme 50
Being Inspired
    as pillar of Readiness for Life programme 50–1
Being a Role Model 193–4
Being a Successful Person 272–3
Belief Labels 89–92
beliefs
    role in aspirations 25

Beliefs About Us 203–6
Believing in Me
    Belief Labels 89–92
    Core Beliefs 80–1
    as curriculum theme in Readiness for Life programme 53–4
    Getting to Know Me 72–3
    Ideal Me 85
    I'm Proud of Me 94
    learning objectives of activities 69
    Locus of Control 76–7, 86–7
    My Beliefs 93
    My Life Map 74–5
    Needs, Success and Aspirations 78–9
    Needs Triangle 88
    as pillar of Readiness for Life programme 51
    Recipe for Success 70–1
    resources for activities 84–94
    Self-Belief 82–3
Bhavnani, R. 29–30
Big Business 254
Borrowing and Lending Cheat Sheet 166–7
Bourdieu, P. 33
Bradley, S. 29
Branding Game, The 258–9
Broecke, S. 30
Budgeting Basics 158, 182–4
Budgets and Profits 252–3, 263, 267–9
Building Skills
    as pillar of Readiness for Life programme 51–2
Bureau of Labor Statistics 13
Business Basics
    Big Business 254
    The Branding Game 258–9
    Budgets and Profits 252–3, 263, 267–9
    Business Case Study 266
    Business Jargon 264–5
    as curriculum theme in Readiness for Life programme 55
    learning objectives for activities 249
    Profit and Loss 257

resources for activities 260–9
SWOT Analysis 255–6
Who Is an Entrepreneur? 250–1, 260–2
Business Case Study 266
Business Jargon 264–5

Cabinet Office 33
Calculating Costs 151–2, 168–9
Career Curves
Career Pros and Cons 218–19
Career Stereotypes 213–14, 225–31
as curriculum theme in Readiness for Life programme 55
A Day in the Life of… 22–12
Gender Stereotypes 215
A Job for Life 210, 224
Job Profiles 234–5
Job Role Case Studies 236–7
Job Role Labels 242–7
learning objectives of activities 207
The Path to Success 222–3, 248
resources for activities 224–48
Skills for the Job 220–1
Types of Work 216–17, 232–3
The World of Work 208–9
Workplace Skills Labels 238–41
Career Pros and Cons 218–19
Career Stereotypes 213–14, 225–31
Certificate of Achievement 294
citizenship
and Readiness for Life programme 48
Clarke, J. 30
Common Inspection Framework 47
communities
role in aspirations 21–3
Core Beliefs 80–1
Cost of Living, The 156–7, 180–1
Crawford, C. 29
Creative Visualisation 134–5, 140–1
cultural capital 33–4
cultural change
definition of 15
and improving aspiration 32–4
Cultural Reproduction and Social Reproduction (Bourdieu) 33

Day in the Life Of…, A 211–12
Deci, E. 40
Department for Business, Innovation and Skills (DBIS) 39
Department for Children, Schools and Families (DCSF) 17, 19, 22

Department for Education (DfE) 29
Department for Education and Skills (DfES) 30
Does Money Matter? 145–6
Dream Building
Creative Visualisation 134–5, 140–1
as curriculum theme in Readiness for Life programme 54
Five Years from Now 136, 142–3
learning objectives of 129
List of Values 138
resources for activities 138–43
Vision Boards 130
Visioning the Future 131–2
Wants versus Needs 133, 139
Duckworth, K. 20

Eccles, J. 20
Estyn 47
ethnicity
and aspirations 29–30

Fawcett Society 27
Feinstein, L. 20
Find Someone 124
First Impressions 110–11, 128
Five Years from Now 136, 142–3
friends
role in aspirations 19–20
Fullan, M. 40

Gates, P. 20
gender
and aspirations 27–8
Gender Stereotypes 215
Getting to Know Me 72–3
Greaves, E. 29
Guardian, The 27
Gutman, I. 18

Hargreaves, A. 40

I Believe in You! 282
Ideal Me 85
Ignition
Being a Successful Person 272–3
as curriculum theme in Readiness for Life programme 55
I Believe in You! 282
learning objectives for activities 270
Personal Mission Statement 286–7
Personal Power 279
The Power Circle 277–8

299

Ignition *cont.*
    Self-Discovery 283, 291
    Self-Talk 280–1
    Sell Yourself 284–5
    Success Profiles 290
    Successful Man 288
    Successful Man Revealed 289
    Universal versus Personal Success 275–6
    Who Is Successful? 274
I'm the Boss 114–15
I'm Proud of Me 94
Influence of the Media, The 188–9
Influences
    Being a Role Model 193–4
    Beliefs About Us 203–6
    as curriculum theme in Readiness for Life programme 55
    The Influence of the Media 188–9
    learning objectives of activities 185
    Limiting Beliefs 195–6
    Mixed Messages 186–7
    Positive Role Models 192
    resources for activities 197–206
    Speech Bubbles 201
    Stereotypes and Labels 190–1, 197–200
    Success Case Study 202
Interview Skills 105

Job Labels 171–4
Job for Life, A 210, 224
Job Profiles 234–5
Job Role Case Studies 236–7
Job Role Labels 242–7
Job and Salary Answers 179

Kintrea, K. 23

Last, K. 20
LearnDirect 149
learning environments
    for Readiness for Life programme 56–8
learning objectives
    of Believing in Me activities 69
    of Business Basics activities 249
    of Career Curves activities 207
    of Dream Building activities 129
    of Ignition activities 270
    of Influences activities 185
    of Money Matters activities 144
    of Skills for Life activities 95
Lewis, G. 30

Limiting Beliefs 195–6
List of Values 138
literacy
    and Readiness for Life programme 47
Locus of Control 76–7, 86–7
Lupton, R. 20, 23

Maslow, A. 37
Maslow's hierarchy of needs 37–8
media
    role in aspirations 20–1
Mixed Messages 186–7
Modood, T. 29
Money Advice Service 150
Money Charity 150
Money Essentials 147–8, 159–63
Money Matters
    Borrowing and Lending Cheat Sheet 166–7
    Budgeting Basics 158, 182–4
    Calculating Costs 151–2, 168–9
    The Cost of Living 156–7, 180–1
    as curriculum theme in Readiness for Life programme 54
    Does Money Matter? 145–6
    Job Labels 171–4
    Job and Salary Answers 179
    learning objectives of activities 144
    Money Essentials 147–8, 159–63
    Money Values 154–5
    resources for activities 159–84
    Salary Labels 175–8
    Savvy Savers 153, 170
    True or False? 149–50, 164–5
Money Values 154–5
MORI/Sutton Trust 19
motivation
    extrinsic 40
    generating self-sustained 40–1
    impacts upon 39–40
    importance of 37
    intrinsic 40
    and Maslow's hierarchy of needs 37–8
    and self-actualisation 37–9
    support for 41–2
My Beliefs 93
My Life Map 74–5

Needs, Success and Aspirations 78–9
Needs Triangle 88
Networking 103
Networking Skills 104

INDEX

Networking Worksheet 123
Nicholls, T. 30
Northwest Regional Development Agency (NWDA) 19, 20, 27, 31–2
numeracy
    and Readiness for Life programme 47

Ofsted 27
Oxford Living Dictionaries 17
Oxford University 27

parents
    role in aspirations 19
Parker, K. 27
Path to Success, The 222–3, 248
Paton, G. 14
Patten, E. 27
peer groups
    impacts on motivation 39–40
    role in aspirations 19–20
Personal Mission Statement 286–7
Personal Power 279
personal social education
    and Readiness for Life programme 48
Pew Research Center 27
Pink, D. 40
Plewis, I. 29
Positive Role Models 192
Potential Employee Case Studies 112–13
Powell, A. 13
Power Circle, The 277–8
Presentation Skills 108–9
Prince's Trust 21
Problem Solving 102, 120–1, 122
Profit and Loss 257
promises in Readiness for Life sessions 61

Quality and Effectiveness Framework 47

Raphael-Reed, I. 20
Readiness for Life (RfL) programme
    aims of 14–15
    assessment of 64–5, 292–3
    Certificate of Achievement for 294
    core features of 45–6
    cornerstones of 15–16
    curriculum links 47–8
    curriculum themes in 49–50, 53–5
    ending 62–3
    and ethnic minority young people 30
    four pillars of 50–2
    impact of 46–7
    learning environments for 56–8
    view of aspiration 17–18
Readiness for Life (RfL) sessions
    behaviour management in 62
    ending 62
    keeping promises 61
    starting 59–60
    tone for 60–1
Recipe for Success 70–1
resources
    for Believing in Me activities 84–94
    for Business Basics activities 260–9
    for Career Curves activities 224–48
    for Dream Building activities 138–43
    for Influences activities 197–206
    for Money Matters activities 159–84
    for Skills for Life activities 112–28

Sabates, R. 20
Salary Labels 175–8
Savvy Savers 153, 170
schools
    role in aspirations 20
self-belief
    impacts on motivation 39–40
    role in aspirations 23–5
Self-Belief (activity) 82–3
Self-Discovery 283, 291
Self-Talk 280–1
Sell Yourself 284–5
skills change
    definition of 15
    and improving aspiration 32–4
Skills for the Job 220–1
Skills for Life
    Agree or Disagree? 106–7, 125–7
    Are You a Team Player? 101, 118–19
    as curriculum theme in Readiness for Life programme 54
    Find Someone 124
    First Impressions 110–11, 128
    I'm the Boss 114–15
    Interview Skills 105
    learning objectives of activities 95
    Networking 103
    Networking Skills 104
    Networking Worksheet 123
    Potential Employee Case Studies 112–13
    Presentation Skills 108–9
    Problem Solving 102, 120–1, 122

Skills for Life *cont.*
    resources for activities 112–28
    Team Building 97–8
    Who Do You Need on Your Team? 100, 116–17
    Who's Right for the Job? 99
society
    impacts on motivation 39–40
    role in aspirations 20–1
Speech Bubbles 201
Stereotypes and Labels 190–1, 197–200
Strand, S. 19, 22
Success Case Study 202
Success Profiles 290
Successful Man 288
Successful Man Revealed 289
Sullivan, A. 33
SWOT Analysis 255–6

Taylor, J. 29
Team Building 97–8

Thoughts, Feelings, Behaviour cycle 24–5
True or False? 149–50, 164–5
Types of Work 216–17, 232–3

Universal versus Personal Success 275–6

Vallerand, R. 41
values
    role in aspirations 25
Vision Boards 130
Visioning the Future 131–2

Wants versus Needs 133, 139
Welsh Government 47
Who Do You Need on Your Team? 100, 116–17
Who Is an Entrepreneur? 250–1, 260–2
Who Is Successful? 274
Who's Right for the Job? 99
Workplace Skills Labels 238–41
World of Work, The 208–9